HOME CANNING AND PRESERVING

PUTTING UP SMALL-BATCH JAMS, JELLIES, PICKLES, CHUTNEYS, RELISHES, SPICES, AND MORE

Janet Cooper

Skyhorse Publishing

Skyhorse Publishing books may be purchased in bulk at special discounts for sales promotion, corporate gifts, fund-raising, or educational purposes. Special editions can also be created to specifications. For details, contact the Special Sales Department, Skyhorse Publishing, 307 West 36th Street, 11th Floor, New York, NY 10018 or info@skyhorsepublishing.com.

Skyhorse® and Skyhorse Publishing® are registered trademarks of Skyhorse Publishing, Inc. ®, a Delaware corporation.

www.skyhorsepublishing.com

10 9 8 7 6 5 4 3 2 1

Library of Congress Cataloging-in-Publication Data is available on file.
ISBN: 978-1-61608-355-7

Printed in China

In memory of
Mary Elizabeth, who taught
Blanche, who taught me

CONTENTS

AUTHOR'S NOTE

This book is intended for the beginning, as well as the experienced, canner who wants to extend the pleasures of pickling, preserving, and making unusual taste treats of all sorts in small batches during any time of the year. A good portion of the recipes can be refrigerated instead of being sealed in jars, which is a boon especially in the winter months when canning supplies are often difficult to find. All of these recipes will provide you with tasty and unusual treats that are perfect to give as gifts. It should be noted that many of the recipes can be safely altered to reflect your own individual taste and preferences. I hope you enjoy expanding your canning and preserving experiences through these small-batch recipes.

EQUIPMENT YOU WILL NEED

Most of the recipes in this collection can easily be made with equipment already in your kitchen but you may want to add a few tools as you go along. Below is a list of the most commonly needed equipment in order to successfully can and preserve just about everything in this book:

- Measuring spoons—metal works best.
- Measuring cups in 1-, 2-, and 4-cup sizes—glass is handiest for measuring liquids and can go in the microwave if necessary. Metal cups are good for sugar and solids.
- Tongs—used to remove boiled jars and lids from boiling water.
- Wide-mouthed funnel—to fit a standard canning jar, preferably metal.
- Sharp knives—buy the best you can afford and also a good sharpener.
- Spoons—an assortment of wood and metal; a flat-ended wooden spoon is a great help when stirring a hot bubbling pot, and a slotted spoon is also useful for straining.
- For breaking up hard spices, such as cinnamon sticks and pepper corns, a tool such as a metal meat-tenderizing mallet will help. A hammer covered with a cloth will work too.
- Vegetable brush—keep it just for food use.
- Grater—one with a variety of hole sizes.
- Juicer
- Ladle for filling jars—a long-handled measuring cup or a teacup will work as a substitute but remember, it will get hot.
- Jar lid tightener—a variety of them is on the market from a useful nonslip pad to a metal gripper.
- Hot pads
- Dishcloths
- Hand and dish towels
- Apron—boiling kettles do spit and fruit juices will stain your clothing.
- Paper towels
- Cheesecloth or muslin and string to make spice bags. A tea caddy will make a good substitute, but you may not want to use it for tea again.
- Jelly bag—the corner of an old pillowcase works well.
- Bowls—a variety of sizes in glass, plastic, or stainless steel.
- Saucepans—stainless steel with a good heavy bottom is best since thin-bottomed pans stick. Aluminum pans will pit from the acid in many foods.
- Colander—such as you would use to drain pasta.
- Diffuser—a variety is available and will be a big help in avoiding stuck and burned mixtures.

canning if you do not want them in the finished product. If left in, there will be some addition of flavor. A large tea caddy will work too and is easy to reuse. To some extent, whole and ground spices are interchangeable. A teaspoon of whole spice is equal to about ¼ to ½ teaspoon ground depending on the bulk of the spice. Some experimentation will be necessary when substituting whole for ground (or vice versa). Unless otherwise noted, ground spices are used in these recipes.

Sugar: Acts as both a preserving agent and a thickener. Be sure to use the amounts stated so you get the intended result, especially in the jam and jelly recipes using liquid or powdered pectin. White and brown sugars will give different flavors. Feel free to experiment, but since brown sugars will seem to be a bit sweeter, start with a little less when experimenting. Other sweetening agents such as corn syrup and artificial sweeteners are best left for recipes designed just for their use.

STEPS IN CANNING: THE OPEN KETTLE METHOD

Probably the most crucial step in canning is getting the food properly into the jars. Done wrong, your jars will not hold a seal and the food will spoil. Two things are essential for a successfully sealed jar: heat and a clean sterile jar. Without heat, a vacuum will not form to hold the lid tightly to the jar rim and the lid will not stick to a jar rim with any food on it. By following these basic steps of the open kettle method, you should have no trouble successfully filling and sealing your jars.

1. Prepare the jars:
   a. Wash the jars carefully and drain.
   b. Inspect the top rim of each jar and do not use chipped or cracked jars, as they will not seal.
   c. Sterilize the jars by either boiling, completely submerged, for 10 minutes or by placing the jars in a 225°F oven for at least a half hour. Jars must be at boiling temperature (212°F) or the temperature of the food when they are filled to avoid cracking. If you do not have soft water for boiling, it is better to sterilize your jars in the oven.
2. Prepare the food to be canned according to the recipe.
3. Sterilize the lids inside the rims by boiling them for 10 minutes while the food is cooking. If that time is up before the food is done, lower the heat and return the lids to a boil before using. Soft water works best for this use.
4. Heat the funnel, tongs, cup, or ladle by placing them in the pan with the lids. They need to be hot to avoid a temperature difference, which could crack the hot jars.
5. When food is ready to can, fill and seal one jar at a time unless otherwise directed. Heat is essential so have all equipment ready to use before starting:
   a. Use tongs to remove two jars from the pan or oven and set them on a heat-proof surface. If the food is not at a boil, let the jars cool a bit before filling to avoid cracking the glass.
   b. Place the hot funnel on a jar and using a ladle or cup, fill the jar to within a half inch of the top. Use a clean spoon to remove excess food if necessary.
   c. Put the funnel and cup on the second jar while sealing the first so any drips will go into that jar. A ladle can go back into the pan or on a saucer.
   d. Use an absolutely clean, damp cloth to wipe the top rim of the filled jar. Any trace of food can cause seal failure. A paper towel will work for this when a small number of jars are to be sealed.

e. Use the tongs to remove a lid and rim from the boiling water. Place them on the jar and screw on tightly. Use a hot pad to hold the jar and another to cover the top. A lid tightening device will help here. Your may need to experiment to find the system that works best for you.

f. Place the sealed jar on a heat-proof surface to cool but keep it out of drafts. Too rapid cooling can cause jars to crack.

g. Before filling the second jar, use the tongs to remove another jar from the kettle or oven and repeat the sealing process.

6. When the jars are completely cool, check them for their seal. Press the center of the lids, which should have been sucked inward at the center and are not flexible. The rims can now be removed for storage or left on. Label the jars, including the date for easy identification of leftovers when next year's jars are stored. A marking pen will write well on the lids. Store the jars upright in a cool dark place since light and heat can cause darkening over time. Do not freeze the sealed jars. Should any jars not be sealed, store them in the refrigerator and use promptly.

STEPS IN CANNING: THE HOT WATER BATH METHOD

~⁓⊙⌀⊙⁓~

Some mixtures do not have enough acid or sugar to be safely canned by the open kettle method. For these you will need to use the hot water bath method. This method requires either a special large kettle with a lift-out rack, usually enamel ware, or a smaller kettle with a rack on the bottom that is deep enough so the jars will be covered by at least one inch of water. For this you will also need strong tongs for lifting the finished jars from the water.

1. Fill the kettle about ½ to ⅔ full of hot water, preferably soft water, cover, and place it over high heat. Also have an extra pan of boiling water ready to fill the canner after the jars are in the water.

2. Prepare the food and fill the jars as the recipe directs:
   a. Hot pack—food is partly cooked before packing into the jars. Then boiling liquid is added to fill the jar to within ½-inch of the top.
   b. Cold or raw pack—uncooked food is packed into jars and then the jars are filled to within ½-inch of the top with boiling liquid.
   c. Syrups for fruit, hot or cold pack:
      • Very light—1 cup sugar, 4 cups water
      • Light—2 cups sugar, 4 cups water
      • Medium—3 cups sugar, 4 cups water
      • Heavy—4 to 4 ¾ cups sugar, 4 cups water
   When filling the jars, be careful not to pack food too tightly and to work out air bubbles. These can cause loss of liquid during processing if a siphoning action begins.

3. Use an absolutely clean wet cloth to wipe off the jar rims.

4. Cover each jar with a sterilized lid and rim. Screw on securely.

5. As each jar is sealed, place it on the wire rack that is suspended over the top of the large water bath kettle. This will start warming the jars and help avoid broken jars. If a conventional kettle is used, place the jars on the rack in the bottom or in a warm oven until all jars are sealed. Boil the water in a separate kettle and pour over the filled jars when all are filled. Jars should not touch each other.

6. When all jars are full, slowly lower the rack into the water. The entire bottom of each jar should hit the boiling water at once. Add boiling water to cover the jars by 1 to 2 inches. Put the lid on the kettle.

7. Return the kettle to a full boil and start timing for the length of time the recipe directs. Adjust the heat to keep the kettle at a boil. If boiling stops, stop timing and resume when the kettle returns to a boil.

8. When the time is done, slowly lift the rack out of the kettle and set it on a folded towel to drain. Wipe the top of each jar. Place the dry jars on a heat-proof surface, out of drafts, to cool. Use tongs to remove the jars from a conventional kettle. Check all jars to be sure the lids are tight.

9. Jars are sealed when the lid is depressed in the center. If a jar does not seal, either refrigerate and use or repeat the processing. Reprocessing is not recommended for cucumber pickles and soft fruits.

JAM

THE LIQUID FRUIT PECTIN METHOD

Few fruits contain enough of the natural jelling agent, pectin, to make thick jams without long periods of cooking. This lack can easily be avoided by adding either natural pectin-rich fruit juices such as apple, currant, or lemon, or by adding commercial pectin such as "Certo," available in grocery stores. By following these basic steps, you can make a wide variety of jams, but it is always best to check the directions on the brand of pectin you are using and to stick with one that gives you consistently good results. Remember that a runny jam makes excellent dessert topping, so there are, in effect, no failed jams.

STRAWBERRY JAM: THE BASIC JAM MAKING STEPS

To most jam makers, sparkling red strawberry jam is the very essence of summer, but with fresh strawberries now available all year round, strawberry jam can be made whenever you wish. As with all fresh fruit, use slightly or just fully ripe berries since riper fruit contains more liquid and less natural sugar, which can result in a runny jam. In winter, it may be necessary to purchase extra fruit to ensure having enough at the right stage of ripeness all at once. The steps in making this jam serve as an example for all jams made with liquid pectin and should be followed for all the recipes in this chapter.

1. Prepare the fruit—wash, pat dry, and hull about two quarts of firm berries. Crush them completely, one layer at a time. A potato masher works well for this.
2. Measure 3 ¾ cups crushed berries and their juice into a large saucepan or kettle. The jam will boil up as it cooks so use a good-sized pan.
3. Add to the pan:
   a. 7 cups (3 pounds) of white sugar
   b. ¼ cup lemon juice (fresh is best)
4. Place the pan, uncovered, on a cold stove, turn the heat high, and bring to a full rolling boil, stirring continually. Boiling fruit will rise up in the pan very rapidly, so watch carefully.
5. Lower the heat slightly and boil hard for one minute, stirring continually. Foam will develop on the surface. Carefully spoon this off into a saucer and save to spread it on bread later for a special treat. It will not hurt the jam if you keep it in the pan, but it will not make as pretty a finished jar.
6. Remove the pan from the heat and at once stir in ½ bottle of pectin or one pouch from a two-pouch box.
7. Stir the jam and skim off foam for 5 minutes. The foam will partially dissolve by itself as the jam cools, but for appearance's sake, it should be removed.
8. Gently ladle the jam into sterile jars and seal at once.

   Yield: 8 to 10 half-pint jars of jam

   TIP: Using the steps in this example, you will be able to make a wide variety of jams. Just use these proportions of fruit and sugar to develop your own special treats:
   About 3 ¾ cups prepared fruits
   ¼ cup lemon juice to add natural pectin
   About 6 to 7 cups sugar
   ½ bottle or one pouch liquid pectin (some recipes will need twice this amount, so read carefully)

APRICOT JAM FROM DRIED APRICOTS

Ingredients:
½ lb. dried apricots
¼ cup lemon juice
7 cups sugar

1. Wash and drain the dried apricots, and place in a saucepan with 3 ¾ cups water. Leave to soak at room temperature for at least 4 hours, or overnight.
2. When soaking is complete, simmer in the pan, covered, for about 30 minutes to soften and break up the fruit.
3. Measure 3 ¾ cups of the fruit and place in a large pan. Add water if there is not enough fruit. If large pieces of fruit are not wanted, cut up the apricots before cooking or mash when soft.
4. Add the lemon juice and sugar. For a taste variety, use orange juice in place of part of the water for cooking or add some finely grated lemon or orange rind.
5. Follow the basic jam-making steps and add 1 whole bottle of pectin or 2 pouches.

Yield: approximately 8 half-pint jars of jam

ORANGE MARMALADE

Ingredients:
5 medium seedless oranges
1 medium lemon
1 grapefruit (optional—this will make a bitter marmalade, which you may prefer)
¼ teaspoon baking soda
6 cups of sugar
½ bottle or 1 pouch liquid pectin

1. Using a vegetable peeler, thinly remove the colored part only of 3 to 4 oranges and the lemon. If using a grapefruit, also remove its peel. The amount of grapefruit rind used will determine the bitterness of the marmalade. As much as possible, avoid any of the white pith of all the fruits.

2. Using a very sharp knife, slice the peels into thin shreds, as narrow as you like. Put the shreds into a pan and add 1 ½ cups water.
3. Add ¼ teaspoon baking soda.
4. Bring to a boil, cover, and cook slowly for 10 minutes.
5. Using a sharp knife, cut the fruit from the membrane by cutting along each side of every section. Work over a bowl to catch the juice and also squeeze the juice from the membranes. If using grapefruit, substitute some grapefruit for some of the oranges if desired. It will alter the flavor of the finished jam.
6. Chop the fruit or, for a smoother marmalade, whir in a blender or food processor. Transfer the fruit and juices to a large pan along with the drained shredded peel. Cook at a slow boil, uncovered, for 20 minutes.
7. Measure 3 cups of this mixture into a large pan. It there is too much, continue to boil until reduced. If too little, add a bit of water.
8. Add the sugar and cook 5 minutes, stirring continuously.
9. Add the liquid pectin. Follow the basic jam-making steps and seal in sterile jars.

Yield: 7 to 8 half-pint jars of marmalade

STRAWBERRY PINEAPPLE JAM

Ingredients:
10 OZ. BOX OF FROZEN, WHOLE STRAWBERRIES, OR 1 CUP CRUSHED FRESH
    STRAWBERRIES
20 OZ. CAN CRUSHED PINEAPPLE PACKED IN JUICE
¼ CUP WATER
3 ½ CUPS SUGAR
1 BOTTLE OR 2 POUCHES LIQUID PECTIN

1. Thaw the frozen strawberries. Thoroughly crush the berries in their juice. Measure 1 cup, including the juice, and put into a large pan or use the fresh berries. Save any extra for another use.
2. Drain the pineapple well and use the juice for something else if desired. Add the pineapple to the berries.
3. Add the water and sugar to the mixture.
4. Follow the basic steps in jam-making and seal in sterile jars.

Yield: approximately 5 ½ half-pint jars of jam

BANANA BUTTER

Ingredients:

8 TO 10 RIPE BANANAS (SHOULD BE SOFT BUT NOT BLACK)

6 CUPS SUGAR

JUICE OF 1 LARGE LEMON

1 BOTTLE OR 2 POUCHES LIQUID PECTIN

1. Crush the bananas to a pulp with a potato masher or use a food processor or blender being careful not to overprocess and incorporate excess air. Crush part of the bananas at a time and measure as you go along. A quart glass measure works well for this. You will need 1 and ½ lbs. of processed fruit, and this is one place where weighing helps (a pound is around a pint measure). Put the crushed fruit in a large pan.
2. Add the sugar and lemon juice.
3. Heat slowly, stirring constantly, until boiling and the sugar has dissolved. Cook at a rolling boil for 1 minute.
4. Add the pectin and follow the basic steps in jam-making and seal in sterile jars.

Yield: about 5 half-pint jars of jam. However, this will vary by the ripeness of the fruit.

*Optional: Add grated citrus fruit rind to taste.

FROZEN UNCOOKED BLUEBERRY JAM

Ingredients:

3 12-OZ. PACKAGES OF FROZEN BLUEBERRIES

5 CUPS SUGAR

¼ TEASPOON CINNAMON

1 BOTTLE OR 2 POUCHES LIQUID PECTIN

2 TABLESPOONS LEMON JUICE

1. Thaw the blueberries. Crush the berries with a potato masher, one layer at a time, measuring as you go (should yield about 4 ½ cups of crushed fruit). Put the fruit into a bowl or large pan. Fresh berries will work too, but be sure they are ripe.
2. Add the sugar and cinnamon. Mix thoroughly and let stand for 30 minutes.
3. In a small bowl, combine the liquid pectin and lemon juice. Stir the pectin into the fruit and stir for 3 to 5 minutes to dissolve the sugar.
4. Ladle into clean freezer containers and cover tightly.

5. Let sit at room temperature about 24 hours or until jellied.
6. Store in the freezer until ready to use. The jam will keep in a refrigerator for 2 to 3 weeks after thawing.

GINGER PEAR JAM

Ingredients:

3 LBS. PEARS, WHATEVER TYPE IS READILY AVAILABLE

1-2 TEASPOONS POWDERED GINGER (ADJUST TO TASTE)

7 ½ CUPS SUGAR

¼ CUP LEMON JUICE

1 BOTTLE OR 2 POUCHES LIQUID PECTIN

1. Peel, remove cores, and grind or chop the pears very finely. A food processor may be used but leave a little texture. Measure 4 cups of fruit and put into a large pan.
2. Add the powdered ginger, sugar, and lemon juice. Mix well and bring to a full rolling boil for 1 minute.
3. Add the liquid pectin. Follow the basic steps for jam-making and seal in sterile jars.

Yield: 8 to 10 half-pint jars of jam

*Optional: Vary the spices with cinnamon, cloves, and allspice to taste. For a more spicy taste, substitute vinegar for the lemon juice.

JAM
THE BOILED METHOD

Using this method will give you the most chances for improvisation but it will take longer since the fruit mixture must be boiled to thicken. The proportions of fruit and sugar will vary but usually it is about 1 cup of sugar for each cup of fruit. You can test for sweetness after the jam has cooked a while by quickly chilling some in the freezer and tasting. More sugar or lemon juice can then be added if needed. The addition of lemon juice will often aid in the jelling process when using low-acid fruits. Jams made using the boiled method go by a variety of names such as conserve and butter as well as just jam. Some may include nuts or raisins. The yield of all these jams will be determined by how much fruit you use, how long it is cooked, and how thick you want the finished jam. After making one of these jams, it will be helpful if you make a note of your yield for future use. Any yields given for these jams are only approximate.

Steps for the basic boiled method:

1. Prepare the fruit as the recipe directs or as you wish.
2. In a large pan, combine the sugar and the fruit.
3. Slowly bring the mixture to a boil, stirring constantly until the sugar is dissolved.
4. Cook at a low boil, stirring often, until the desired thickness is reached. This is a useful place to have a flat-ended wooden spoon and to use a diffuser. A good test is to put a little on a small saucer, place it in the freezer, and cool to see how thick it is when cold.
5. Remove from the heat and skim off any foam.
6. Seal in sterile jars.

APPLE GINGER JAM

Ingredients:

3 LBS. TART COOKING APPLES, SUCH AS MCINTOSH

2 ½ CUPS WATER OR FRESH APPLE CIDER

¾ CUP SUGAR PER CUP OF FRUIT

2 SMALL LEMONS, RINDS FINELY GRATED AND JUICE

4 OZ. CRYSTALLIZED GINGER, FINELY CHOPPED, OR 1 TEASPOON POWDERED GINGER

1. Wash, core roughly, and cut up the apples. Put them in a large kettle and add the water or fresh cider. Cook until the apples are very soft and breaking up. Strain the apples, measure, and return to the kettle.
2. Add ¾ cup sugar per cup of fruit.
3. Add the lemon rind and juice and the ginger.
4. Heat slowly and cook to desired thickness. Seal in sterile jars.

Yield: will depend on how thick you want your jam

*Note: Orange juice used in the initial cooking will give this jam a different taste.

APPLE BUTTER

Ingredients:

8 LBS. RIPE COOKING APPLES, SUCH AS MCINTOSH

WATER OR APPLE CIDER

½ CUP SUGAR PER CUP OF STRAINED APPLES

2 TEASPOONS CINNAMON

½ TEASPOON ALLSPICE

½ TEASPOON CLOVES

1. Wash, roughly core, and cut up the apples. Place in a large kettle and add enough water or cider to come about ⅓ of the way up the apples. Cook until the apples are well done and easily break up. Strain the apples, measure, and return to the kettle.
   Note: One way to speed up the final cooking of the jam is to cook part of the apples, covered, in the microwave along with a very little water. This will reduce some of the liquid after straining and speed the thickening of the jam.
2. Add about ½ cup sugar per cup of strained apples. You may use brown sugar or some of both brown and white if you prefer. It might be good to scant the sugar and taste before adding it all.
3. Add the cinnamon, allspice, and cloves, adjusting the amounts to your taste.
4. Cook over low heat, stirring often, until desired thickness. Seal in sterile jars.

PUMPKIN PIE BUTTER

～✦～

Ingredients:

1 15-oz. can pumpkin (not pie filling)

½ cup brown sugar

½ cup white sugar

4 tablespoons pure maple syrup

1 tablespoon fresh lemon juice

1 teaspoon mixed pumpkin pie spice

1. Mix everything together in a small but deep saucepan. Bring slowly to a boil and then place on a diffuser if possible. Cook very slowly over low heat for ½ hour. Stir often and cover with a lid left slightly ajar to allow steam to escape. This jam will spit badly since it is quite thick to start with.

2. Seal in sterile jars or cool and refrigerate until used.

   Yield: approximately 3 half-pint jars of pumpkin butter

*Note: If you prefer, replace the commercial mixed pumpkin pie spices with ½ teaspoon cinnamon, ¼ teaspoon cloves, and ¼ teaspoon ginger. The maple syrup may be replaced with either honey or sorghum in the same amount or molasses in half the amount plus 2 tablespoons water. The easiest way to measure the sugars is to pack the brown sugar into the bottom of your cup and then fill it with white sugar. The amounts of all the seasoning can easily be altered to suit your taste, so feel free to experiment. This butter is especially tasty eaten on warm corn muffins.

CRANBERRY PEACH JAM

～✦～

Ingredients:

1 17-oz. can sliced peaches in heavy syrup

2 cups fresh cranberries, washed and picked over

1 cup golden raisins

1 cup water

1 teaspoon finely grated orange rind

1 teaspoon finely grated lemon rind

1 cup sugar

½ cup frozen orange juice concentrate, undiluted

1. In a large pan, combine the cranberries and peaches. Drain the peach juice into the kettle and chop or crush the peaches before adding them.
2. Wash the raisins and squeeze them dry before adding to the mixture.
3. Add the water, grated orange rind, and grated lemon rind. Bring slowly to a boil and simmer for 15 minutes, stirring occasionally
4. Add the sugar and concentrate. Return to a boil and simmer, stirring often, until thick, about 30 to 35 minutes. Seal in sterile jars.

Yield: approximately 4 to 5 half-pint jars of jam

*Note: For a smoother jam, crush with a potato masher after step 3 or use an immersion blender. You may use 2 cups of diced fresh peaches instead of the canned fruit. This will alter the cooking time since there will be less liquid to start with though ripe peaches have quite a lot of juice in them.

FRUIT MEDLEY JAM

Ingredients:
FRESH RIPE PEARS, PEELED, CORED, AND CHOPPED
FRESH PEACHES, PEELED, PIT REMOVED, AND CHOPPED
FRESH PLUMS, SEEDS REMOVED AND CHOPPED
SUGAR

1. Crush or whirl in a blender or food processor an equal amount of the pears, peaches, and plums. Measure and place in a large pan.
2. Add sugar measured equal to the measured fruit.
3. Bring slowly to a boil and cook to desired thickness over medium heat.

Yield: 7 to 8 half pints to 6 cups of fruit

*Note: If fresh peaches are not available, you can use peaches canned in juice, draining before adding. If using canned plums, buy them canned in low-sugar and drain well.

CRANBERRY CONSERVE

Ingredients:

4 CUPS FRESH CRANBERRIES

1 ½ CUPS WATER

2 ½ CUPS SUGAR

1 CUP RAISINS, GOLDEN OR DARK, WASHED AND SQUEEZED DRY

1 LARGE COOKING APPLE, SUCH AS MCINTOSH

FINELY GRATED RIND AND JUICE OF 1 LEMON

FINELY GRATED RIND AND JUICE OF 1 ORANGE

1 CUP CHOPPED WALNUTS

1. Wash and pick over the cranberries. They may be chopped in a blender or food processor if a less chunky jam is desired.
2. Add the water and cook the berries at a simmer until fruit is soft and whole berries pop completely.
3. Add the sugar and raisins. Dried currants may be substituted for raisins. They are smaller so will give a less lumpy jam.
4. Peel, core, and chop the apple and add it along with the grated lemon rind and juice and grated orange rind and juice.
5. Cook at a slow boil until desired thickness.
6. Add the chopped walnuts or other nuts of choice. Reheat to boil and seal in sterile jars.

Yield: approximately 8 half-pint jars of jam

*Note: Chopped dried apricots may be added but add additional sugar if you do so. Fruit juice can also be used instead of water to cook the cranberries.

JAM MADE FROM THE PULP LEFT AFTER MAKING JELLY

Ingredients:

JUICE AND PULP FROM JELLY-MAKING RECIPES

1 CUP SUGAR FOR EACH CUP OF TART FRUIT PULP (½ TO ¾ CUP SUGAR FOR A SWEETER PULP)

LEMON JUICE, IF PULP IS EXTREMELY THICK

1. After the juice has been removed for jelly-making, strain the pulp to remove any seeds or lumps. Measure the pulp.
2. Add 1 cup sugar for each cup of tart fruit pulp or ½ to ¾ cup sugar for sweeter fruit pulp.

3. Lemon juice or other fruit juice should be added to extremely thick pulp. If it is too thick, it will burn quickly when cooked.
4. Bring the mixture to a slow boil and simmer, stirring, for at least 10 minutes or until of desired thickness. Seal in sterile jars.

* Note: Spices and other fruits can be added before cooking for a different taste. When using extremely thick pulp, you may need to add a little water or complimentary fruit juice.

SNOW-TIME CONSERVE

Ingredients:
1 ½ CUPS CUT-UP, DRIED PITTED PRUNES
1 ½ CUPS CHOPPED DRIED APRICOTS
WATER, APPLE JUICE, OR ORANGE JUICE
1 SEEDLESS ORANGE
1 8.75-OZ. CAN CRUSHED PINEAPPLE PACKED IN JUICE
5 CUPS SUGAR
¼ CUP LEMON JUICE

1. In a kettle, almost cover the prunes and apricots with water or fruit juice, and simmer, covered, for 10 minutes, or until the fruit is soft.
2. Remove the orange part of the orange peel with a vegetable peeler. Slice the peel into thin slivers. Add to the kettle while the prunes and apricots are cooking. Remove the orange fruit by cutting on each side of every section. Work over a bowl to catch the juice. Chop the fruit and add juice and fruit to the kettle.
3. Chop the canned pineapple in food processor or blender if a smoother jam is wanted. Add to the kettle along with its juice.
4. Add sugar and lemon juice. Mix everything and boil slowly until of desired thickness. Seal in sterile jars.

Yield: approximately 4 to 5 half pints

*Note: A ¼ cup brandy or orange liqueur will add a different taste to this jam. Chopped Maraschino or candied cherries will add more color. For an apricot-only jam, replace the prunes with more apricots. Adding some ginger will give a nice taste to apricot-only jam.

PINEAPPLE JAM

Ingredients:

20 oz. can crushed pineapple packed in juice

1 tablespoon fresh lemon juice

¼ teaspoon ginger (optional)

yellow food coloring (optional)

1 ½ cups white sugar

1. Whirl the pineapple in a blender or food processor until fairly smooth. Leave some texture.
2. Add the lemon juice. If you like, add ginger. For a brighter color to your jam, add a drop of yellow food coloring.
3. Simmer, uncovered, for about 45 minutes until quite thick, stirring occasionally. A diffuser will help.
4. Add the sugar and continue simmering for about 30 minutes until very thick. Stir often. Test for setting. Seal in sterile jars.

Yield: approximately 2 ½ cups

*Note: This is a jam that can easily be personalized by adding other fruits or spices.

PINEAPPLE JAM USING FRESH PINEAPPLE

Ingredients:

1 RIPE PINEAPPLE

BOTTLED UNSWEETENED PINEAPPLE JUICE

¾ CUP SUGAR FOR EACH CUP PUREED FRUIT

¼ TEASPOON GINGER FOR EACH 2 CUPS FRUIT (OPTIONAL)

YELLOW FOOD COLORING (OPTIONAL)

1. Cut off the top of the pineapple and slice in half from top to bottom. Cut each half into at least three sections lengthwise. Lay each piece on its side and slice off the hard core. Cut away the outer rind, being careful to remove all eyes. Next, cut the fruit into small pieces and process in a blender or food processor until fairly smooth. Measure and pour into a large pan.
2. Bring to a boil and simmer, covered, until thick, about 45 to 60 minutes. Add bottled unsweetened pineapple juice as needed and stir occasionally.
3. Add ¾ cup white sugar for each cup of pureed fruit. If you like, add ginger and yellow food coloring to make the jam a brighter color.
4. Return to a simmer and cook uncovered, stirring often, until very thick, about 30 minutes. After cooking for 15 minutes, taste for sweetness and add ¼ cup sugar per cup of fruit if needed. The sweetness of your pineapple will determine the need for extra sugar.
5. Seal in sterile jars.

Yield: will be determined by the size of the pineapple

SWEET CHERRY JAM

Ingredients:
1 ½ LBS. FROZEN, PITTED BING CHERRIES
1 LARGE MCINTOSH APPLE
3 TABLESPOONS FRESH LEMON JUICE
3 ½ CUPS WHITE SUGAR

1. Thaw the frozen cherries completely. Peel, quarter, core, and chop the apple into small pieces. Chop the mixed fruit in a blender or food processor, in batches, until fairly finely chopped but leave some texture. If necessary, add a little water to make processing easier but do not use more than ½ cup in total. There should be about 4 cups of processed fruit at the end. Pour into a large saucepan.

2. Add the fresh lemon juice. Cook, covered, at a strong simmer until fairly thick, about 1 hour. Add the sugar and continue cooking, uncovered, until jam tests for setting by putting a little in the freezer to chill quickly.

3. Seal in sterile jars.

   Yield: approximately 5 half-pint jars of jam

   *Note: After the sugar is added, the jam may be boiled, uncovered, on high heat, but it must be stirred constantly to avoid sticking and burning.

   *To use fresh Bing cherries, start with about 1 ¾ lbs. ripe but still firm cherries, Wash, dry, and remove the pits before chopping enough cherries along with the apple to measure 4 cups.

APRICOT JAM

Ingredients:
7 OZ. BAG OF DRIED APRICOTS
2 CUPS WATER PER CUP OF CHOPPED APRICOTS
1 CUP WHITE SUGAR PER CUP OF FRUIT
1 TABLESPOON FRESH LEMON JUICE

1. Start with dried apricots in whatever quantity you choose. Dice the apricots and measure. One 7 oz. bag will yield about 1 cup chopped apricots.
2. Add 2 cups water per cup of chopped apricots and simmer, covered, about 2 hours until the fruit is very soft and the water is well reduced. Mash with a potato masher or whirl in a blender or food processor until the desired smoothness.
3. Measure the fruit, and for each cup, add 1 cup sugar. Add the lemon juice.
4. Simmer, uncovered, at least 10 minutes or until desired thickness, stirring often. A diffuser under the pan will help avoid sticking. Seal in sterile jars or store in the refrigerator.

Yield: approximately 2 cups jam per cup of chopped apricots

*Note: You may prefer to add the water a cup at a time as the cooking progresses. Interesting additions might be ginger, chopped apples, or other fruits.

APRICOT ORANGE JAM

Ingredients:

7 OZ. BAG DRIED APRICOTS

2 SMALL NAVEL ORANGES

2 CUPS WATER

1 CUP SUGAR FOR EACH CUP COOKED FRUIT

1. Dice the apricots. Quarter the oranges lengthwise, trimming away the thick rind at each end, and slice thinly. Combine the fruit with water in a heavy-bottomed saucepan.
2. Simmer, covered, for about 2 hours until everything is very soft and liquid is well reduced. If there is too much liquid when the fruit is soft, raise the heat and boil, stirring constantly, until reduced. For a smoother jam, mash with a potato masher but leave some texture.
3. Measure the fruit. Return to the pan and add the sugar. Continue simmering until the jam is quite thick and tests for setting. Seal in sterile jars.

Yield: 5 half-pint jars of jam

*Optional: Add ½ teaspoon powdered ginger or more to taste. Puree the apricots and add to the oranges when measuring for sugar. This will leave the orange slices whole, more like marmalade. Adding a chopped cooking apple such as McIntosh will give a milder jam.

PEACH AND ORANGE JAM

Ingredients:

1 ½ LBS. FROZEN SLICED PEACHES

1 NAVEL ORANGE

¼ CUP WATER

1 TABLESPOON FRESH LEMON JUICE

2 CUPS SUGAR

¼ TEASPOON GINGER (OPTIONAL)

1. Thaw the peaches. Shred the orange part of the rind using the next to the largest holes on your grater and put the shreds into a saucepan. Remove the rest of the rind and the outer membrane. Cut between the dividing membranes and remove the fruit sections. Work over a bowl to catch any drips and include any juice squeezed from the membranes.

2. Whirl all the fruit in a blender or food processor in batches until well chopped but not completely pureed. There will be about 3 cups of processed fruit. Place in a saucepan or kettle.

3. Use the water to rinse out the machine and add it along with the lemon juice to the fruit. Cook, uncovered, at a simmer for about 30 minutes until the fruit bits are very soft and the volume is somewhat reduced. Stir often.

4. Add the sugar and, if you desire, the ginger. You can also add chopped Maraschino cherries for extra color.

5. Return to a simmer, stirring, and taste for sweetness. If desired, add up to ½ cup additional sugar. Continue cooking for about 20 minutes and start to test for setting.

6. Seal in sterile jars.

Yield: approximately 4 half-pint jars of jam

*Note: Fresh peaches may be used. Peel, slice, and process enough to measure 3 cups when added to the processed orange.

JAM AND JELLY
THE POWDERED PECTIN METHOD

Powdered fruit pectin is available in small premeasured boxes. They are easy to use and give as good results as liquid pectin. The only difference is that powdered pectin must be added *before* the sugar since it will not dissolve and work properly in a high-sugar solution. The sugar is added last and may be premeasured and warmed in the oven to avoid cooling the jam too much when it is added.

Experimentation is more difficult with powdered pectin since the box is not easily divided. As a result, the amount of fruit and sugar varies with the natural acidity of the fruit. One box will jell 5 to 7 cups of very tart fruit and about 6 to 7 cups of sugar. For sweeter, less acid fruit, use 1 box with 3 to 5 cups fruit and 4 to 6 cups sugar. Some trial and error will be necessary to create your own jams and jellies by this method. Should you not be able to purchase powdered pectin, use these recipes but substitute the liquid pectin and its method.

Basic steps for using powdered fruit pectin:

1. Prepare the fruits as directed by the recipe.
2. Measure fruit into a very large saucepan or small kettle.
3. Measure the sugar and set aside.
4. Mix powdered pectin into the fruit.
5. Place the pan over high heat and stir until mixture reaches a hard boil.
6. Quickly add the sugar.
7. Bring the mixture to a full rolling boil and boil for 1 minute.
8. Remove from the heat, stir for 5 minutes, skimming off any foam that rises to the surface.
9. Seal in sterile jars following the steps in the basic directions on p. 8.

STRAWBERRY JAM

Ingredients:

2 QUARTS FULLY-RIPE BUT STILL FIRM STRAWBERRIES

1 BOX POWDERED PECTIN

7 CUPS SUGAR

1. Wash and hull the strawberries. Crush completely, one layer at a time, using a potato masher. Measure 4 ½ cups into a large pan.
2. Add the powdered pectin. Bring to a hard boil and add the sugar. Follow the basic directions and seal in sterile jars once complete.

Yield: approximately 8 to 10 half-pint jars of jam

APRICOT HONEY JAM

Ingredients:

6 OZ. CONTAINER OF DRIED APRICOTS

2 CUPS WATER

¼ CUP LEMON JUICE

1 BOX POWDERED PECTIN

2 CUPS SUGAR

2 CUPS HONEY

1. Finely chop the dried apricots. Put into a saucepan and add the water.
2. Bring to a boil, reduce heat, and simmer, covered, until fruit is very soft. For a smoother jam, crush the fruit with a potato masher. Measure fruit and, if necessary, add water to make 3 cups. Pour into a large pan.
3. Add the lemon juice and the pectin.
4. Once at a hard boil, add the sugar and honey.
5. Follow the basic directions and seal in sterile jars once complete.

Yield: approximately 6 half-pint jars of jam

FIG JAM

Ingredients:
½ LB. DRIED FIGS
¼ CUP LEMON JUICE
1 BOX POWDERED PECTIN
4 ½ CUPS SUGAR

1. Remove any stems from the dried figs and grind or chop very finely. Add water to make 3 and ½ cups. Pour into a large pan and simmer, covered, until the fruit is soft
2. Add the lemon juice and pectin. Bring the mixture to a boil.
3. Once the mixture has reached a hard boil, add the sugar.
4. Follow the basic instructions and seal in sterile jars once complete.

Yield: approximately 6 half-pint jars of jam

*Note: Some finely grated orange rind would make a nice addition to this jam.

CUCUMBER LIME JAM/JELLY

Ingredients:

½ cup lime juice

¼ cup cider, white wine or rice wine vinegar

2 limes

1 long English cucumber, peeled, seeded, and chopped

¼ teaspoon salt

green food coloring (optional)

1 box powdered pectin

4 cups sugar

1. Finely grate the rind from the whole limes, juice them, and combine all the juice, rind, and vinegar in a blender or food processor. While the machine is running, keep adding pieces of cucumber. Blend until the mixture is smooth and measure 4 cups in all.
2. Pour into a kettle. For a clear jelly, you will need to strain the mixture through a jelly bag and add water and a little more lime juice to make 4 cups.
3. Add salt. If you want a greener jam/jelly, add a few drops of green food coloring.
4. Pour in the box of pectin and bring the mixture to a hard boil. Once boiling, quickly add the sugar.
5. Follow the basic instructions and seal in sterile jars once complete.

Yield: 5 to 6 half-pint jars

*Note: For a different taste, add some snipped fresh dill weed or some dried dill along with the salt.

RHUBARB GINGER JELLY

Ingredients:

3 quarts of fresh or frozen chopped rhubarb

water

2 teaspoons ground ginger, or to taste

red food coloring (optional)

1 box powdered pectin

5 ½ cups sugar

1. If using frozen rhubarb, thaw and chop before measuring. Place the fruit in a large pan and add enough water to almost cover. Boil until very soft and strain through a jelly bag for several hours or overnight. Measure 5 cups of the juice, adding a little water if needed. Put it into a kettle.
2. Add ground ginger. If you want a brighter-colored jelly, add a few drops of red food coloring.
3. Add the box of pectin and bring to a hard boil. Once boiling, quickly add the sugar.
4. Follow the basic instructions and seal in sterile jars once complete.

Yield: 8 to 10 half-pint jars of jelly

*Note: Just before sealing the jars, sprinkle a bit of ginger on top or float a thin slice of peeled fresh ginger in the middle of each jar. Lemon juice may replace a little of the water for cooking the rhubarb

AN ASSORTMENT OF JELLIES MADE WITH POWDERED FRUIT PECTIN

❦

All of these jellies are made using one box of powdered fruit pectin, so just the amount of juice and sugar are listed. Follow the steps for making jelly with powdered pectin on p. 29.

1. Tangerine Jelly
   - 3 cups canned unsweetened tangerine juice
   - 5 ½ cups sugar
2. Grapefruit Jelly
   - 4 cups canned unsweetened grapefruit juice
   - 5 cups sugar
3. Cider Jelly
   - 4 cups fresh apple cider
   - 4 ½ cups sugar
   - 1 or 2 tablespoons fresh lemon juice
4. Wine Jelly
   - 4 cups of your favorite dry wine, white or red
   - 6 cups sugar
5. Cranberry Jelly
   - 3 cups cranberry juice cocktail
   - 4 cups sugar
6. Mint Apple Jelly
   - 3 ¾ cups bottled apple juice
   - ¼ cup lemon juice
   - A few drops of green or yellow food coloring (optional)
   - 1 cup loosely packed fresh mint leaves or 2 tablespoons dry
   - Heat juices just to a boil, add mint, and let steep at least 30 minutes
   - Strain through a fine sieve and make jelly adding 4 ½ cups sugar
   - This jelly is nice served with roast lamb
7. Port and Grape Jelly
   - ½ cup bottled grape juice
   - 1 ½ cups port wine
   - 1 cup water
   - 3 cups sugar

JELLY
THE LIQUID PECTIN METHOD

There is little difference between making jam and making jelly. Jellies are usually clear with no pieces of fruit and generally have a stiffer texture. When jellies are made with bottled juices, you eliminate the need to strain cooked fruit through a jelly bag, which speeds up the process. When making jellies using liquid pectin, the steps are the same as when making jam (see p. 11), so in some cases, only ingredients are listed in the recipes below.

GRAPE JELLY

Ingredients:

4 CUPS BOTTLED CONCORD GRAPE JUICE, OR THE SAME AMOUNT MADE FROM FROZEN
      CONCENTRATE MIXED WITH SLIGHTLY LESS WATER THAN USUAL

7 CUPS SUGAR

½ BOTTLE OR 1 POUCH LIQUID PECTIN

Yield: 5 to 6 half-pint jars of jelly

WINE JELLY

Ingredients:

2 CUPS WINE, WHATEVER TYPE YOU PREFER

3 CUPS SUGAR

½ BOTTLE OR 1 POUCH LIQUID PECTIN

1. Measure the sugar and wine into a large pan. Cook, stirring, over medium heat until mixture is just below the boiling point. Continue stirring until sugar is dissolved, about 5 minutes, but do not boil.
2. Remove from the heat and at once stir in the pectin. Mix well and skim off the foam. Quickly pour into sterile jars and seal.

Yield: approximately 4 half-pint jars of jelly

HERB JELLY

This jelly serves as a good accompaniment for meats.

Ingredients:
2 ½ cups water
4 tablespoons dried herbs, or 1 cup fresh herb leaves and stems, of your
    choosing
¼ cup cider vinegar, wine vinegar, apple juice, or water
4 ½ cups sugar
yellow or green food coloring (optional)

1. Begin with an herb infusion: Boil the water and stir in the dried or fresh herbs, lightly packed. Use whatever herbs you prefer or a mixture of several. Cover and let stand for 15 minutes or as long as overnight for a stronger taste. Strain through a fine sieve and measure 2 cups into a large pan.
2. Add the liquid of your choice (cider vinegar, wine vinegar, apple juice, or water) and the sugar. If you want a brighter color, add a few drops of yellow or green food coloring.
3. Follow the steps for making jam with liquid pectin using a ½ bottle or 1 pouch of pectin.

Yield: 5 to 6 half-pint jars of jelly

*Note: If using fresh herbs, a leaf may be floated in the center of each jar before sealing. If a sharper taste is desired, add a few drops of hot pepper sauce to the infusion before cooking the jelly. A few slices of lemon or orange rind removed with a vegetable peeler can be added when soaking the herbs. A different taste will result from adding a few thin slices of onion when making the infusion. This is a good recipe for experimentation.

RASPBERRY JELLY

Ingredients:

1 LARGE BAG FROZEN, UNSWEETENED RASPBERRIES

¾ CUP WATER

6 CUPS SUGAR

1 BOTTLE LIQUID PECTIN

1. Thaw the bag of raspberries completely and crush the berries one layer at a time or whir in a blender or food processor. Scoop the mashed berries into a jelly bag—the corner of an old pillowcase works for this. Tie the filled bag tightly and suspend from a cupboard door over a kettle for several hours or overnight. Do not squeeze the bag as this can cloud the juice. When the bag has thoroughly stopped dripping, measure 3 cups into a large pan. Add water if necessary to make this amount.

2. Add water—may be part lemon juice—and sugar. Pour in 1 whole bottle of liquid pectin.

3. Follow the basic directions on p. 8 and seal in sterile jars once complete.

    Yield: approximately 6 half–pint jars of jelly

    *Note: The fruit left in the bag may be strained to remove the seeds. Sweeten and use as dessert topping or add spices and a little vinegar to use as a relish.

WATERMELON JELLY

Ingredients:

3 1-LB. PACKAGES OF CUBED WATERMELON (OR YOU MAY USE FRUIT LEFT OVER FROM MAKING WATERMELON RIND PICKLES, P. 122)

7 ½ CUPS SUGAR

JUICE OF 1 LEMON

SEVERAL DROPS OF RED FOOD COLORING

2 POUCHES LIQUID PECTIN

1. Cut up, remove seeds, and puree the watermelon in a food processor or blender. Strain overnight through a cloth bag or a large sieve lined with damp paper towels. For jelly, you will want crystal-clear juice.
2. In a large pan, combine 4 cups of watermelon juice, the sugar, lemon juice, and a few drops of red food coloring to give it a rosier color.
3. Follow the basic steps for making liquid pectin jelly.

Yield: approximately 9 half–pint jars of jelly

WATERMELON SORBET

Ingredients:

WATERMELON JUICE (LEFT OVER FROM OTHER RECIPES)
¼ CUP OF SUGAR FOR EACH CUP OF JUICE
1 TABLESPOON FRESH LEMON JUICE

1. In a bowl, for every cup of watermelon juice, add ¼ cup sugar. Add the lemon juice. Stir to dissolve the sugar and let stand for 30 minutes, stirring often and then chill.
2. Place the covered bowl in the freezer and let freeze until almost set. Whip with an electric beater and return to the freezer to freeze completely.
3. Two hours before serving, re-beat and return to the freezer. Further beating is not necessary for leftovers.

*Note: The sorbet can be made in an electric ice cream maker following the directions that come with the machine.

JELLY
THE BOILED METHOD

Jellies made by this method are a bit tricky. It is easy for them to end up either slightly rubbery or else runny. So be sure to test for jelling and be prepared for some interesting ice cream toppings along the way, but the results of a well-jelled jelly are most yummy and worth the effort. The yield of these jellies will vary depending on how long they are cooked. On the average, you will have around 1 cup of jelly for every 12 ounces of juice.

The basic boiled method for jelly:

1. Prepare the fruit as the recipe directs.
2. After it is cooked, drip the juice through a jelly bag for several hours or overnight. Do not squeeze the bag. It is easiest to hang the bag from a cupboard door over a kettle or bowl.
3. Measure the juice into a large pan. Add sugar and cook at a low boil, stirring often, until the jelly sets.
4. Test for jelling by putting a bit in the freezer to quickly chill. Set the pan aside while doing this. Jelly will usually set at 220 to 222°F on a candy thermometer. Another sign is when two drops form at the edge of a large metal spoon and then run together to form a sheet while they fall. At this point, turn off the heat and skim off any foam.
5. Seal in sterile jars. Pulp left from jelly-making can be made into jam or spiced fruit (see p. 53).

CRANBERRY JELLY

Ingredients:

4 CUPS CRANBERRIES

¾ CUP SUGAR FOR EACH CUP OF JUICE

1. Cook the cranberries in 3 cups water until very soft. Chopping them first will speed the cooking.
2. Strain the juice through a jelly bag. Measure the juice and add ¾ cup sugar for each cup of juice. Bring to a boil, stirring, and boil to the jelling point.
3. Seal in sterile jars.

LEMON JELLY

Ingredients:

6 LEMONS

7 ½ CUPS WATER

2 ¼ CUPS SUGAR FOR EVERY 2 ½ CUPS JUICE

YELLOW FOOD COLORING (OPTIONAL)

1. Slice the lemons thinly, remove the seeds, and put the fruit into a large pan along with the water. Tie the seeds in a small cloth and add to the pan. The seeds will add extra natural pectin. Bring to a boil and then simmer, covered, for 1 ½ hours.
2. Strain the juice through a jelly bag. Squeeze the bag of seeds into the jelly bag. Measure the juice and return it to the cleaned kettle.
3. Add 2 ¼ cups of sugar for every 2 ½ cups of juice or a scant cup of sugar to each cup of juice. You may add several drops of yellow food coloring for a brighter jelly.
4. Follow the basic method and seal in sterile jars.

Yield: will depend on the size of your lemons

*Note: A nice addition would be a clean sprig of parsley or a basil leaf suspended in each jar. Be sure to wash and dry the herb first.

POMEGRANATE JELLY

Ingredients:
6 VERY RIPE POMEGRANATES
JUICE OF 2 ORANGES
FINELY GRATED PEEL AND JUICE OF 1 LEMON
SUGAR

1. Remove the juice sacks from the pomegranates and mash them, one layer at a time, or whir in a blender or food processor.
2. Add the juice from the oranges, the grated lemon peel, and the lemon juice. Bring the juices to a boil and simmer, covered, for 10 minutes.
3. Strain the juices through a jelly bag. Measure and add an equal amount to water. In a kettle, bring to a boil and simmer for 20 minutes, uncovered.
4. Let cool enough to measure and add an amount of sugar equal to the reduced juice. Boil to the jelling point and seal in sterile jars.

*Note: Add a few drops of red food coloring if jelly appears pale. Cut thin slices of lemon or orange rind with a vegetable parer and float one in each jar of jelly for eye appeal.

TANGERINE JELLY

Ingredients:

8 TANGERINES
1 LARGE LEMON
SUGAR

1. Wash the tangerines and lemon, and cut off thin strips of rind with a vegetable peeler. Shred the peel into thin slivers and set aside. Remove all of the white rind and outer membrane. Cut the fruit from the membranes by cutting along the sides of each section. Squeeze juice from the membranes and discard them. Remove seeds from the fruit and tie in a cloth. Chop the fruit by hand or in a blender or food processor.

2. Simmer the fruit, juices, shredded peel, and seeds, covered, for 15 minutes. Strain through a jelly bag overnight.

3. Measure the juice and pour into a kettle. Add an equal amount of sugar and slowly bring to a boil.

4. Cook at a low boil to the setting stage and seal in sterile jars.

TANGERINE JAM

Ingredients:

LEFTOVER PULP FROM TANGERINE JELLY RECIPE, PREVIOUS PAGE

SUGAR

¼ CUP WATER FOR EVERY CUP FRUIT

JUICE OF 1 LEMON

YELLOW FOOD COLORING (OPTIONAL)

1. Measure the pulp left from the tangerine jelly in a quart-size measure. Squeeze the seed bag into a kettle and discard the seeds. Add the fruit to the kettle.
2. Add an amount of sugar equal to the measured fruit (scant a little for less sweet jam) and ¼ cup water for every cup fruit. Also add the juice of one lemon and, if desired, a few drops of yellow food coloring for added color.
3. Heat slowly, stirring, and then boil to the setting point as for jam or until desired thickness.
4. Seal in sterile jars.

TRADITIONAL
MARMALADES

Sparkling bitter-orange marmalade is expensive and hard to duplicate at home since the bitter Seville oranges are hard to find and have a short season. If this is the only type of marmalade you like, be resigned to purchasing it most of the time. However, the addition of grapefruit rind to your marmalade will go a long way toward the bitter marmalade taste. If the clear taste of sweet navel oranges and other citrus fruits appeals to you, you will find the time involved in making your own traditional marmalades is well worth the results. The varieties you can make are only limited by your imagination. The following set of directions may appear complicated, but since the process is spread over three days, the time spent each day is not so long. It is a basic framework for making any type of citrus marmalade in any quantity, so let your imagination run wild.

Day One

1. Use a single type of citrus fruit or a variety. Wash and dry the fruit. Remove just the colored layer of rind with a vegetable peeler and slice it into shreds with a sharp knife or kitchen shears. Process as much rind as you wish and set it aside. If you are using a variety of fruits, you may want to use an equal amount of each or to emphasize just one. Put any unshredded rind into a large kettle.
2. Remove all the white pith and outer membrane from all the fruit, working down to the exposed fruit. Add the pith to the large kettle with the unshredded rind.
3. Cut the fruit from the dividing membranes by cutting on each side of every section with a sharp knife. Work over a bowl to catch any juice and put the fruit into that bowl. Squeeze the juice from the membranes into the bowl. Add any seeds and the membranes to the kettle with the pith.

4. Chop the fruit or whirl in a blender or food processor. How finely the fruit is chopped will determine the texture of the finished marmalade. Add the shredded rind to the chopped fruit and measure it all together.

5. Put the fruit into a large pan and measure the water—three times the amount of fruit. Pour some of that water over the pith and add the rest to the fruit. Bring both mixtures to a boil, remove from the heat, cover, and let stand for 24 hours. You now have two working kettles: one holding the fruit and shreds and the other with the pith and seeds.

*Note: The reason for processing the pith and seeds is that much of the natural pectin in citrus fruit is located there. It is extracted this way to help the marmalade set. The extra rind is included to add its natural flavor oils, and any fruit left on the membranes will also add flavor.

Day Two

1. Bring both kettles to a boil and simmer, covered, for 15 minutes. Remove from heat, cover, and let stand for another 24 hours.

*Note: This extra day's soaking is not included in many recipes. In fact, many do not call for a soaking at all. Soaking does seem to mellow the flavor, especially of blended marmalades, and it does soften the rind. Boiled marmalades that have not been soaked will need to be aged for at least a week or two to let the flavor develop. Since very little of your time is involved, why not let your marmalade soak twice? It can't hurt.

Day Three

1. Drain the water from the pith and add to the fruit. Tie the pith and seeds in a cloth bag and add that to the fruit also. Bring the kettle to a boil and cook at a slow boil, uncovered, for 1 to 2 hours. The amount should be reduced by one-half and the shredded rind should be tender. Squeeze all liquid from the bag of pith back into the kettle with the fruit. Discard the pith and seeds.

2. Measure the fruit mixture and add an equal amount of sugar. Heat slowly, stirring constantly. When the sugar is dissolved, bring the jam to a boil and cook at a slow boil until the desired thickness. Test for thickness as for boiled jam. This last cooking will take between 10 and 30 minutes depending on the type of fruit used.

3. Remove the kettle from the heat and stir for 5 minutes to cool slightly and prevent floating rind. Seal in sterile jars. If the marmalade is not to be sealed for storage, allow the kettle to stand for 24 hours and stir again before storing in clean containers in the refrigerator. This will more evenly distribute the rind.

Many variations of these basic steps will result in interesting and individual marmalades. After making a variety of pure citrus marmalades, you might like to try some additions:

- A chopped peeled apple will soften the flavor.
- Chopped candied ginger makes a pleasant addition.
- A tablespoon or so of dark molasses will give a darker, richer color while some green food coloring will perk up the appearance of lime marmalade.

Let your imagination go, have fun, and create your own private blend.

ENGLISH MARMALADE

Ingredients:
2 LBS. SEVILLE OR BITTER ORANGES
1 LARGE LEMON
WATER
8 CUPS SUGAR

Day One

1. Remove the ends of the oranges and lemon and cut them in quarters lengthwise. Remove the seeds and slice the fruit as thinly as possible with a sharp knife.
2. Measure everything and put it in a large kettle. Add an equal amount of cold water, stir, cover, and let stand for 24 hours.

Day Two

1. Bring the kettle to a boil.
2. Remove from the heat, stir well, cover, and let stand for 24 hours.

Day Three

1. Bring the jam to a boil. Add the sugar. Stir until the sugar is dissolved and simmer, uncovered, for 2 hours, stirring often. A diffuser under the pan will help avoid sticking.
2. When the peel is transparent and soft, bring to a rapid boil and cook about 30 minutes. Test for setting and continuing cooking until that point is reached.
3. Let stand a few minutes, skim, and seal in sterile jars.

Yield: approximately 7 to 8 half-pint jars of marmalade, depending on the size of the fruit

LIME MARMALADE—A ONE-DAY MARMALADE

Ingredients:

12 LIMES

7 ½ CUPS WATER

SUGAR

GREEN FOOD COLORING

1. Remove the green part of the lime rind with a vegetable peeler and shred it thinly with a sharp knife. Process as much rind as you wish. Cut away all the white pith and outer membranes and discard them. Remove the fruit from between the membrane and squeeze any juice from the membranes. Discard the membranes and pith.

2. Remove the seeds from the fruit and tie them in a cloth. Chop the fruit or whirl in a blender or food processor.

3. Put the fruit, juices, and bag of seeds in a large kettle. Add the water and simmer for 1 hour, uncovered. Remove the seed bag and squeeze out the juices.

4. Measure the fruit and juices and add an equal amount of sugar and a drop or two of green food coloring. Bring to a boil, stirring, and boil rapidly for about 15 minutes.

5. Start testing for jelling, and when thick enough, seal in sterile jars.

Yield: approximately 10 half-pint jars of marmalade, depending on the size of the limes

EXTRA: FRUIT COMBINATIONS FOR INTERESTING MARMALADES

❧

All of these are one-day marmalades. With each mixture, before adding the sugar, measure the fruit mixture. After adding the sugar, slowly return the jam to a boil and cook at a slow boil to the setting point, stirring often. The yield from these recipes depends on the size of the fruit used and any additions you may make. On the average, you will get about 10 to 12 ounces of marmalade for every 8 ounces of cooked fruit measured before adding sugar.

CRANBERRY PINEAPPLE MARMALADE

❧

Ingredients:

3 CUPS CRANBERRY JUICE COCKTAIL

1 STANDARD-SIZED CAN CRUSHED PINEAPPLE PACKED IN JUICE, AND ITS JUICE

2 LARGE LEMONS

SUGAR TO EQUAL THE COOKED FRUIT

1. Remove the large ends of the lemons, cut into quarters lengthwise, remove any seeds, and slice crosswise very thinly. An orange may also be added. Treat the same as the lemons.
2. Simmer for 1 hour in the juice and pineapple. Cool enough to measure and then add an equal amount of sugar. Follow the basic steps and seal in sterile jars once complete.

APPLE MARMALADE

❧

Ingredients:

1 NAVEL ORANGE

1 SMALL LEMON

6 MEDIUM-SIZED APPLES (ANY TYPE OF COOKING APPLE THAT WILL HOLD ITS SHAPE
   WILL DO)

2 CUPS WATER OR COMPLIMENTARY JUICE

SUGAR

1. Remove the large ends of the orange and lemon, cut in quarters lengthwise, remove seeds, and thinly slice crosswise. Peel, core, and chop the apples as small as you wish. Add water or a complimentary juice. More liquid may be needed during cooking.
2. Simmer everything for about an hour, stirring often. Cool enough to measure and then add an equal amount of sugar. Follow the basic instructions and seal in sterile jars once complete.

APRICOT LEMON MARMALADE

Ingredients:

DRIED APRICOTS

1 MEDIUM LEMON FOR EACH CUP OF CHOPPED DRIED APRICOTS

1 CUP OF WATER FOR EACH CUP OF CHOPPED APRICOTS

SUGAR

1. Chop the apricots and measure them. Slice the lemons as in the Apple Marmalade recipe (see above) or treat them as in the English Marmalade recipe (p. 48).
2. Add 1 cup of water for each cup of chopped apricots (more may be needed during cooking). Simmer everything for about 45 minutes or until the lemon rind is soft.
3. Measure and add an equal amount of sugar. Follow the basic instructions and seal in sterile jars once complete.

SPICED
FRUITS

These sauces differ little from boiled jams, and the steps taken to make them are practically the same. Any type of fruit can be made into a tasty spiced sauce by adding some vinegar and a selection of spices. The texture of your finished sauce will be determined by the fruit you use, so for a smoother sauce, just whir the fruits in a blender or food processor before cooking or after they are soft. When whole spices are used, they can be left in the finished product or removed, but leaving them in will allow a little more flavor to develop over time. These sauces are a wonderful treat with meats or by themselves used as jam. You can easily customize your sauce by adding other fruits and spices, so feel free to experiment. Your yield will depend on how much fruit and other ingredients you use, but it will be about 10 to 12 ounces of sauce for every 8 ounces of everything measured before adding sugar.

SPICED CRANBERRY SAUCE

Ingredients:

4 cups cranberries

¼ cup cider vinegar

1 cup water or ½ cup water and ½ cup orange juice

1 teaspoon cinnamon

½ teaspoon cloves

finely grated rind of 1 orange

2 cups sugar (half may be white and half brown)

1. Wash and pick over the cranberries, removing any soft berries. For a smoother sauce, chop the cranberries in a blender or food processor before cooking.

2. Combine all the ingredients in a pan and bring to a boil, stirring. Cook at a low boil, uncovered, for 10 minutes.
3. Add the sugar, return to a low boil, and cook until thick, stirring often. Seal in sterile jars.

Yield: approximately 3 to 4 half-pint jars

SPICED FRUIT SAUCE MADE FROM THE PULP LEFT AFTER MAKING JELLY

Ingredients:
LEFTOVER PULP FROM ANY JELLY RECIPE

For each cup of strained pulp:
1 CUP SUGAR
¼ TO ¼ CUP CIDER VINEGAR
¼ TEASPOON CINNAMON
¼ TEASPOON CLOVES
GINGER AND ALLSPICE TO TASTE
WATER OR COMPLIMENTARY FRUIT JUICE (ONLY AS NEEDED)

1. Strain and measure the pulp. Put in a large pan and for each cup, add the above measurements of sugar, cider vinegar, cinnamon, cloves, ginger, and allspice. Additional liquid may be needed, so use water or a complimentary fruit juice.
2. Cook to desired thickness and seal in sterile jars.

SPICY LEMON MARMALADE

Ingredients:

4 LARGE LEMONS

1 SEEDLESS ORANGE

¼ CUP CIDER VINEGAR

¾ CUP WATER

1 CUP SUGAR PER CUP OF FRUIT

¼ TEASPOON POWDERED GINGER PER CUP OF FRUIT, OR TO TASTE

1. Prepare the fruit as for marmalade (see p. 46). Measure the fruit and shredded peels, and for each cup, add the above measurements for cider vinegar and water.
2. Let the mixture sit, covered, overnight in a pan large enough for cooking the next day.
3. On day 2, boil the fruit and liquids until the peel is tender, measure, and add the sugar and powdered ginger to taste using the above measurements. Bring to a boil slowly and cook at a low boil to the jelly stage. Seal in sterile jars.

*Note: Altering the spices will give you a different taste experience. Some other spices to consider are cardamom, cloves, and curry powder.

SPICED DRIED CURRANTS

Ingredients:

1 11-OZ. BOX DRIED CURRANTS

¾ CUP WATER OR ORANGE JUICE

1 ORANGE

¾ CUP CIDER VINEGAR

¾ TO 1 CUP BROWN SUGAR

¼ TEASPOON CINNAMON

¼ TEASPOON ALLSPICE

¼ TEASPOON CLOVES

1 TO 2 TABLESPOONS BRANDY OR RUM (OPTIONAL)

1. Wash the currants in warm water, pick over for any stems, drain well, and squeeze dry. Place in a saucepan. Add the water or orange juice and several thin slices of orange rind removed with a vegetable peeler.

2. Cook slowly, covered, for 1 hour or until almost dry. A diffuser on the burner will help avoid scorching.

3. Remove the rind and add the cider vinegar, brown sugar, finely grated rind from the rest of the orange cinnamon, allspice, and cloves. Cook slowly, covered, for ½ to 1 hour, or until the desired consistency. The mixture will thicken when cold. If you are adding brandy or rum, stir in now.

*Note: This makes a small batch of currants, so storing in the refrigerator is probably best. They will keep very well that way. They can also be sealed in sterile jars but you will have less than a pint unless the recipe is multiplied. Raisins may be used instead of currants. They should be chopped first.

SPICED PINEAPPLE SAUCE

Ingredients:

20 OZ. CAN CRUSHED PINEAPPLE PACKED IN JUICE

1 CUP SUGAR (HALF WHITE AND HALF BROWN, IF DESIRED)

1 TEASPOON GINGER

¼ TEASPOON ALLSPICE

¼ TEASPOON CLOVES

⅛ TEASPOON GROUND BLACK PEPPER (OMIT FOR A LESS SPICY SAUCE)

1 SMALL LEMON, JUICED (ABOUT ¼ TO ⅓ CUP)

FINELY GRATED LEMON RIND (OPTIONAL)

1. Drain the pineapple and collect the juice. There will be about 1 cup of juice. In a medium saucepan, boil the juice down, uncovered, to ½ cup, about 10 to 15 minutes. Add the rest of the ingredients, except the fruit, to the juice.

2. Bring the pan slowly back to a boil, stirring to dissolve the sugar. Let cook at a slow boil for 3 minutes. Add the fruit and let cook, uncovered, at a slow boil until thick. The juices will be thick and syrupy and the temperature will be about 218 to 220°F. Cooking will take around 30 to 45 minutes. Stir often and constantly at the end since the mixture will easily stick as it thickens.

Yield: will depend on how long the sauce is cooked but it should be about 1 pint

*Note: If you prefer to start with a fresh pineapple, choose one that is ripe but not incredibly soft. Remove the skin and hard core. Chop the fruit into small pieces by hand or in a blender or food processor in several batches. Strain the fruit, and if there is more than ½ cup of juice, boil it down to ½ cup. The rest of the recipe will be about the same, though the cooking will probably take longer. The fruit should become soft. Taste your mixture when it has cooked for 15 minutes and add additional seasoning if necessary. A large pineapple may need more of everything. There is no vinegar included in this recipe. If you prefer the taste, add 2 tablespoons of cider vinegar to the juice before boiling it down to ½ cup.

SPICED APPLE SLICES

Ingredients:

5 LARGE COOKING APPLES, SUCH AS JONATHAN, THAT WILL KEEP THEIR SHAPE WHEN COOKED

2 CUPS WHITE SUGAR

2 STICKS CINNAMON, BROKEN

1 CUP VINEGAR

2 TEASPOONS WHOLE CLOVES

1 CUP WATER OR FRUIT JUICE

RED FOOD COLORING

1. Peel, quarter, and core the apples. Cut in fairly thick wedges, lengthwise.
2. Combine the sugar, cinnamon sticks, vinegar, whole cloves, water or fruit juice, and several drops to red food coloring and heat to boiling. Let simmer, covered, for 15 minutes. Allowing the syrup to steep overnight will add to the flavor.
3. Return the syrup to a boil. Add the apple wedges and cook gently in several batches until barely tender but not broken. Put cooked apples in an oven-proof bowl and keep hot in a 220°F oven while cooking more. Additional food coloring may be needed as you go along.
4. Pack the apples in sterile jars, add boiling syrup, and seal or store in the refrigerator.

Yield: depends on the size and type of apples, about 2 to 3 pints

SPICED RED GRAPE SAUCE

Ingredients:

RED SEEDLESS GRAPES

1 MCINTOSH APPLE

1 CUP SUGAR

2 TABLESPOONS CIDER VINEGAR

GRATED RIND AND JUICE OF ½ LEMON

¼ TEASPOON CLOVES

¼ TEASPOON ALLSPICE

1. Wash and cut in half enough grapes to measure 2 cups, packed. Try to buy them as sweet as possible. Wash, peel, core, and cut up the apple. Chop both fruits together in a blender or food processor until quite finely chopped but leave some texture. Pour into a saucepan.

2. Add the sugar, cider vinegar, grated lemon rind, lemon juice, cloves, and allspice. Stir well and bring to a boil, stirring until the sugar dissolves. Then, lower the heat and simmer until quite thick or about 210°F. This will take about 1 to 1 ½ hours depending on the amount of juice in the grapes. Seal in sterile jars.

Yield: approximately 2 cups

*Note: Start with the 2 tablespoons vinegar and taste after partly cooked. If more is desired, add it by the tablespoon. Also, due to the high water content of these grapes, cooking time is quite long. To speed this up, boil the fruit alone, quite hard, for 10 to 15 minutes, stirring often. Then, add the remaining ingredients and cook at a simmer. If you can find black seedless grapes, try this recipe with them also.

SPICED WHOLE PRUNES

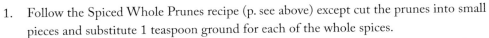

Ingredients:

2 LBS. WHOLE, PITTED PRUNES

2 CUPS BROWN SUGAR

1 CUP CIDER VINEGAR

2 LARGE STICKS CINNAMON, BROKEN

1 TABLESPOON WHOLE CLOVES

1 SMALL LEMON

1. Wash the prunes and drain well.
2. Make a syrup by combining the brown sugar, cider vinegar, cinnamon sticks, and whole cloves in a pan large enough to hold the prunes. Wash and remove the large ends from the lemon, cut in half lengthwise, slice thinly crosswise, and remove seed. Add to the pan.
3. Bring to a boil, stirring, and simmer, covered, for 30 minutes.
4. Add the prunes and simmer until just soft but still holding shape. Seal in sterile jars.

Yield: approximately 3 pint jars

SPICED PRUNE SAUCE

1. Follow the Spiced Whole Prunes recipe (p. see above) except cut the prunes into small pieces and substitute 1 teaspoon ground for each of the whole spices.
2. Cook until thick. For a smooth sauce, whir in a blender or food processor or force through a sieve. Return to a boil, stirring continuously, before sealing in sterile jars.

The yield will be less than it is for the whole fruit.

SPICED MIXED DRIED FRUITS

Ingredients:

6 CUPS DRIED FRUIT OF YOUR CHOICE

WATER OR FRUIT JUICE

¾ CUP SUGAR

2 STICKS CINNAMON, BROKEN

1 TEASPOON DRIED CRACKED GINGER, OR 1 PIECE WHOLE DRIED GINGER, BROKEN UP

1 TEASPOON WHOLE CLOVES

1 ½ CUPS RESERVED FRUIT LIQUID

1 SMALL LEMON OR ORANGE

1. Select a total of 6 cups of dried fruits of your choice, keeping each type separate since they will need different cooking times. Wash each fruit and put in a separate pan with just enough water or fruit juice to almost cover. Cook at a slow boil, covered, until almost soft but still holding shape. Drain each fruit and reserve all the juices together in a separate container. Place all the fruit in a bowl as it finishes cooking.

2. When the fruits are all cooked, in a separate pan large enough to hold the fruit, make a syrup by combining the sugar, cinnamon, dried cracked ginger, whole cloves, 2 cups of the reserved fruit liquid, and lemon or orange (cut in half and thinly sliced crosswise after removing the seeds).

3. Simmer the syrup slowly, covered, until the lemon or orange rind is getting soft. Add the cooked fruit to the syrup and simmer, uncovered, until fruit is soft but still holding shape, about 10 to 15 minutes. More liquid may be needed if the fruits absorbed a lot while cooking.

4. Seal in sterile jars.

Yield: will vary depending on the type of fruit used but should be around 3 pint jars

*Note: If you want a more of a pickle taste, add ¼ cup cider vinegar to the syrup and boil it uncovered.

SPICED DRIED FRUIT BUTTER

1. Cook the selected fruits as for the Spiced Mixed Dried Fruits recipe (see above) but cook until well done and almost falling apart.

2. Force the fruits through a sieve or whir in a blender or food processor and put in a pan along with 2 cups of their juices.

3. Add the syrup ingredients substituting ½ teaspoon ground cinnamon for the whole sticks and ¼ teaspoon ground spice for whole cloves and ginger. Taste and add more of the spices if you wish. Add the grated rind of 1 lemon or orange instead of the whole fruit. The juice of the fruit may also be added but your sauce will need longer cooking due to the added liquid.

4. Slowly bring to a boil, stirring constantly, and cook until thick. Seal in sterile jars.

SPICY ORANGE SLICES

Ingredients:
8 SEEDLESS NAVEL ORANGES
WATER
4 CUPS SUGAR
1 CUP VINEGAR
½ CUP ORANGE COOKING LIQUID
1 TEASPOON WHOLE CLOVES
2 LARGE CINNAMON STICKS, BROKEN
½ TEASPOON BROKEN DRIED WHOLE GINGER ROOT

1. Wash, dry, and remove a slice from each end of the oranges. Slice them about ¼ inch thick. Oranges may be cut in half lengthwise before slicing if you prefer. In a large pan, barely cover the slices with water and cook, covered, at a simmer until the rinds are tender. This may take an hour or so. Drain and reserve the liquid.

2. Make a syrup with the sugar, vinegar, orange cooking liquid, whole cloves, cinnamon sticks, and ginger root. Combine all syrup ingredients and slowly bring to a boil, stirring. Cook at a slow boil, uncovered, until quite syrupy.

3. Add the oranges, stir gently, and let stand overnight. The next day, bring to a boil, simmer slowly for 10 minutes, and seal in sterile jars.

Yield: approximately 3 pint jars

SPICY ORANGE SAUCE

1. After cooking and draining the oranges as in the Spicy Orange Slices recipe (see p. 61), process in a blender or food processor until as smooth as you wish. When making the syrup, substitute 1 teaspoon ground cinnamon for the sticks and ¼ to ½ teaspoon ground for the cloves and ginger.

2. Add the processed fruit to the syrup and simmer until the desired thickness. Seal in sterile jars. There will be a smaller volume to the sauce than with the slices.

*Note: Most of these spiced fruit sauces can easily be converted into jams by omitting the vinegar and spices. They are then boiled to the setting stage for jam. Converting to chutney is also easy. Add some finely chopped onion, perhaps more spices and fruits, and cook until thick.

CHUTNEY

Chutney is just another version of boiled jam with additional spices, onions (typically), and possibly other vegetables. These sauces were traditionally served with Indian and Far Eastern dishes but now we know they make a very tasty addition served with any meat or poultry dish. Boiled jams and spiced fruits can easily be turned into chutney by adding some chopped onion and more spices before cooking. Traditional chutneys are usually quite spicy but not necessarily hot, so for additional heat, add more ginger and pepper to any type of chutney. Chutney can be a smooth sauce or have more texture, so either leave fruits in small chunks or whir it in a blender or food processor. Your yield from these recipes will depend on how thick you want the sauce and any other ingredients you may add as well as the type of jars you choose. Any yields given are only approximate, so always sterilize a few extra jars "just in case."

APPLE CHUTNEY

Tis is a mild chutney.

Ingredients:

4 LBS. APPLES, ANY TYPE

3 MEDIUM YELLOW OR WHITE ONIONS

2 ½ CUPS VINEGAR

1 ½ CUPS JUICE (ORANGE, APPLE, CIDER, OR A COMBINATION)

1 TABLESPOON GINGER

1 TEASPOON ALLSPICE

1 TEASPOON NUTMEG

1 TEASPOON CLOVES

¼ TEASPOON CAYENNE PEPPER

2 CUPS BROWN SUGAR

2 CUPS DRIED CURRANTS OR RAISINS

1. Peel, core, and dice the apples. Peel and finely chop the onions.
2. Add the vinegar, juice, ginger, allspice, nutmeg, cloves, and cayenne pepper. Mix well and cook, uncovered, at a simmer or until thick.
3. Add the brown sugar. Wash and squeeze dry the currants or raisins and add. Cook everything until desired thickness and seal in sterile jars.

Yield: 5 to 6 pint jars

APRICOT ORANGE CHUTNEY

Ingredients:
Use the Apricot Orange Jam recipe on p. 126 and replace ½ cup of the water with cider vinegar or to taste

Additional ingredients:
1 small onion
½ cup currants, washed
½ teaspoon powdered ginger
¼ teaspoon cloves
¼ teaspoon allspice

1. Prepare the chutney and cook as in the recipe on p. 64. Finely chop the onion and cook with the fruit for the last hour.
2. When sugar is added, include the currants, powdered ginger, cloves, and allspice.
3. Chutney is a sauce, so stop cooking when thick but not as thick as jam.

Yield: see left

*Note: If you do not want the chutney as sweet as jam, reduce the amount of sugar added to taste. Start with ½ cup for each cup of fruit, taste when dissolved, and slowly add sugar as wanted, remembering that the hot mixture will taste sweeter than the chilled sauce. The amount of vinegar can also be adjusted to your taste. For hot chutney, add minced hot pepper to taste along with the onion or add powdered red pepper along with the spices.

LEMON CHUTNEY

Ingredients:

4 LEMONS

2 ROME APPLES

2 MEDIUM YELLOW OR WHITE ONIONS

1 CUP DRIED CURRANTS

½ CUP RAISINS

3 CUPS CIDER VINEGAR

2 CUPS WATER, AS NEEDED

3 TEASPOONS POWDERED GINGER

2 TEASPOONS POWDERED ALLSPICE

1 TEASPOON POWDERED CLOVES

¼ TEASPOON POWDERED RED PEPPER

¼ TEASPOON POWDERED GARLIC

3 CUPS SUGAR

1. Juice the lemons first and then cut up the rinds, discard the seeds and membranes. Peel the apples, remove the cores, and cut into small chunks. Peel and cut the onions into small chunks. Wash and squeeze dry the currants and raisins. Mix everything together and grind.
2. Place the ground fruit in a heavy-bottomed saucepan and add the vinegar, water, garlic, ginger, allspice, cloves, and red pepper.
3. Mix well; bring to a boil and simmer, covered, for 1 ½ hours, stirring often. A diffuser will help avoid sticking. If the mixture becomes too think, add water a little at a time and stir well.
4. Stir in the sugar and continue simmering 1 hour, stirring often. Seal in sterile jars.

    Yield: 4 to 5 pint jars of chutney

*Note: For more texture, leave the currants whole. Remove the lemon rinds in strips, cut the fruit from between the membranes, and roughly chop, saving any juices. Grind the rinds but not the fruit. For hotter chutney, cut up a hot pepper and grind with the fruits. A whole fresh garlic clove may be ground or minced instead of using powdered. Other forms of ginger may be used instead of powdered. Fresh ginger or candied ginger should be either ground or minced very finely before being added. Some experimentation will be necessary to determine how much of these you prefer to use.

SUNSHINE CHUTNEY

This is a mild chutney.

Ingredients:
4 LARGE ORANGES
1 LARGE APPLE
½ CUP GOLDEN RAISINS
½ CUP VINEGAR
1 ½ CUPS WATER OR JUICE
1 TABLESPOON CURRY POWDER
½ TEASPOON GINGER
½ TEASPOON CINNAMON
¼ TEASPOON CLOVES
1 ¼ CUPS SUGAR

1. Grate the orange rind and remove the white pith and outer membrane. Cut the fruit from between membranes and dice, keeping the juice. Peel and dice the apple.
2. Combine all ingredients. Simmer about 1 hour or until desired thickness.

Yield: approximately 5 half-pint jars of chutney

SIX-FRUIT CHUTNEY

❦

This is a mild chutney.

Ingredients:

½ CUP CRUSHED PINEAPPLE, DRAINED

1 LIME

2 TART APPLES

1 FIRM BUT RIPE PEAR

1 NAVEL ORANGE

2 CUPS FRESH CRANBERRIES

1 ½ CUPS WATER, PINEAPPLE JUICE, CIDER, OR ORANGE JUICE

½ CUP VINEGAR

½ TEASPOON CURRY POWDER (COMMERCIAL OR SEE P. 192)

½ TEASPOON GINGER

½ TEASPOON CLOVES

¼ TEASPOON CAYENNE PEPPER

1 TO 2 CUPS SUGAR

½ CUP CURRANTS OR RAISINS

¼ CUP WALNUTS, CHOPPED

1. Cut the lime in quarters lengthwise, remove seeds, and slice thinly crosswise, discarding the ends without fruit. Peel, core, and dice the apple and pear. Grate the orange rind; remove all pith and outer membrane. Cut the fruit from between the membranes. Squeeze the juice from the membrane before discarding it. Chop the fruit, keeping any juice. Wash and chop the cranberries either by hand or in a blender or food processor.

2. Combine the fruits along with the water or juice, vinegar, curry powder, ginger, cloves, and cayenne pepper. Simmer 30 minutes to 1 hour, uncovered, until line rind is somewhat transparent and softened. Add additional liquid, a little at a time, if the mixture becomes too dry.

3. Add the sugar and currants or raisins, which have been washed and squeezed dry. Continue cooking to desired thickness and add the walnuts. Seal in sterile jars.

Yield: approximately 2 pint jars

RHUBARB APPLE CHUTNEY

This is a mild chutney.

Ingredients:

2 LBS. FROZEN RHUBARB OR FRESH, IF AVAILABLE

3 CUPS COOKING APPLES, FINELY CHOPPED OR GRATED

½ CUP YELLOW ONION, FINELY CHOPPED

1 CUP CURRANTS OR CHOPPED RAISINS

1 ORANGE

2 ½ CUPS BROWN SUGAR, OR HALF WHITE SUGAR

½ CUP CIDER VINEGAR

1 TEASPOON GINGER

1 TEASPOON ALLSPICE

½ TEASPOON CLOVES

½ TEASPOON CINNAMON

1. Chop or cut the rhubarb into small pieces. Add the apples, onion, and currants or raisins. Grate the orange rind fairly coarsely, remove all the pitch, and cut the fruit from the membrane. Chop the fruit and add along with any juice from the membranes. Stir in the remaining ingredients.

2. Mix well and cook, slowly, until thick, about 1 hour. Seal in sterile jars.

Yield: approximately 3 to 4 pints

CRANBERRY CHUTNEY

❧

This is a mild chutney.

Ingredients:
1 STANDARD-SIZED CAN WHOLE CRANBERRY SAUCE
½ CUP RAISINS OR CURRANTS
½ CUP CHOPPED DATES (FIGS MAY BE SUBSTITUTED IF DESIRED)
⅓ CUP CHOPPED YELLOW OR WHITE ONION
½ CUP SUGAR, WHITE OR BROWN
½ CUP CIDER VINEGAR
½ TEASPOON GINGER
½ TEASPOON CINNAMON
¼ TEASPOON ALLSPICE
¼ TEASPOON CLOVES
⅛ TEASPOON BLACK PEPPER

1. Wash, squeeze dry, and chop the raisins and add to the cranberry sauce. If using currants, leave them whole. Add the chopped dates, finely chopped onion, sugar, vinegar, spices, and pepper.

2. Cook slowly until thick, about 30 minutes. Stir often. Seal in sterile jars or refrigerate.

Yield: 2 to 3 half-pint jars of chutney

CRANBERRY CHUTNEY 2

This is a mild chutney.

Ingredients:
1 12-oz. bag fresh cranberries
1 orange
¼ cup yellow onion, minced
1 cup brown sugar
1 cup water
⅓ cup cider vinegar
½ cup currants
½ teaspoon cinnamon
½ teaspoon cloves
½ teaspoon ginger

1. Wash and pick over the cranberries very carefully and measure about 3 cups whole berries. Coarsely grate just the outer orange rind. Remove all the white pith and cut the fruit from between the membranes. Squeeze the juice from the membranes. Chop the cranberries and orange in a blender or food processor
2. Add the minced onion, sugar, water, vinegar, washed currants, and spices.
3. Simmer, uncovered, for about 1 hour or until thick. Taste after 30 minutes and adjust seasonings if more are wanted. Seal in sterile jars.

Yield: approximately 4 cups

*Note: Other fruits, such as apple and apricots, would be a nice addition to this chutney. Use a cooking apple such as McIntosh and chopped dried apricots. A half-cup washed and squeezed currants can be added to the chopped fruit. For a spicier chutney, add some cayenne pepper to taste.

PEACH CHUTNEY

～⚬∽⚬◦～

This is a medium chutney.

Ingredients:

2 STANDARD-SIZED CANS SLICED PEACHES IN LIGHT SYRUP

1 SMALL ONION, FINELY CHOPPED

1 CUP SUGAR, WHITE OR BROWN

1 CUP CIDER VINEGAR

½ CUP JUICE FROM THE PEACHES

¾ CUP RAISINS OR CURRANTS

2 TABLESPOONS MINCED CRYSTALLIZED GINGER

½ TEASPOON CLOVES

¼ TEASPOON ALLSPICE

¼ TEASPOON CAYENNE PEPPER OR MORE TO TASTE

1. Drain the peaches well and chop, saving the juice. Add the onion, sugar, vinegar, juice from the peaches, chopped raisins (or washed and squeezed dry currants, if using), ginger, spices, and pepper.

2. Cook slowly until thick, about 1 hour, and seal in sterile jars.

Yield: approximately 2 pints

*Optional additions: 2 cloves garlic, minced; coarsely-grated rind; and juice of one lemon or orange

*Note: For a hotter chutney, increase the amount of pepper. Other canned fruits, such as apricots, may be used instead of or in addition to the peaches. Fresh peaches may be used instead of the canned. You will need about 3 cups of diced fruit. Some orange juice will replace the canned juice.

DRIED FRUIT CHUTNEY

T his is a medium chutney.

Ingredients:
½ LB. DRIED PEACHES
½ LB. DRIED APRICOTS
½ LB. DATES
½ LB. RAISINS OR CURRANTS
1 LB. TART APPLES
2 CLOVES GARLIC
2 CUPS SUGAR
1 TEASPOON ALLSPICE
1 TEASPOON CLOVES
1 TEASPOON GINGER
¼ TEASPOON CAYENNE PEPPER OR GRIND A HOT PEPPER OF CHOICE WITH THE FRUITS
2 CUPS VINEGAR
1 CUP OF A COMPLIMENTARY FRUIT JUICE OR WATER

1. Chop the fruits and garlic. Mix together and grind. A food processor might work but you want a fairly smooth paste when done.
2. In a kettle, combine fruit, with the sugar (more for a sweeter sauce), spices, pepper, vinegar, and fruit juice or water. Mix carefully and, stirring often, cook slowly, uncovered, until thick and soft, about 30 to 45 minutes. Seal in sterile jars.

Yield: approximate 4 to 5 pints

*Note: Fruits may be chopped instead of ground, which will determine the texture of the finished chutney and its cooking time. Instead of the dried peaches and apricots, you may substitute 1 lb. assorted dried fruits of your choosing.

RIPE MANGO CHUTNEY

This is a medium chutney.

Ingredients:

5 LARGE RIPE MANGOS
½ CUP RAISINS OR CURRANTS
1 SMALL ONION
1 TABLESPOON MUSTARD SEED
1 TABLESPOON MINCED FRESH GINGER ROOT
1 CUP BROWN SUGAR
½ CUP CIDER VINEGAR
½ CUP FRESH LIME JUICE FROM 2 OR 3 WHOLE LIMES
¼ TEASPOON CRUSHED, DRIED CHILI PEPPERS OR MORE TO TASTE
1 CLOVE GARLIC

1. Pare the mango and cut the fruit into small pieces. Chop the raisins (currants may be left whole), and peel and finely chop the onion. Mix together in a kettle with the mustard seed and the peeled and finely chopped ginger root. Add the brown sugar (using more for a sweeter chutney). Set aside.
2. In a blender, puree the vinegar, lime juice, chili peppers, and garlic clove (peeled and chopped or crushed).
3. Combine all ingredients in the kettle with the fruit, mix well, cover and let stand overnight.
4. On day 2, bring slowly to a boil, stirring, and cook at a simmer for about 3 hours, or until fruit is soft and the mixture is thick. If the mixture gets too dry before it is done, add a little juice as needed. A diffuser on the burner will help avoid sticking and burning. If you prefer a smoother sauce, use a potato masher to smooth out any large lumps but leave some texture.

Yield: approximately 3 pints

DRIED FRUIT AND ORANGE CHUTNEY

This is a medium-hot chutney.

Ingredients:

1 CUP PACKED, CHOPPED MIXED DRIED FRUIT

1 CUP RAISINS OR CURRANTS

1 SMALL ONION

1 ORANGE

1 LARGE GARLIC CLOVE, OR ¼ TO ½ TEASPOON POWDERED GARLIC

2 CUPS WATER OR JUICE SUCH AS ORANGE OR APPLE JUICE OR CIDER

1 TABLESPOON GINGER

½ TEASPOON CLOVES

½ TEASPOON ALLSPICE

¼ TEASPOON CAYENNE PEPPER OR MORE TO TASTE

1 TABLESPOON PREPARED HORSERADISH (WITHOUT CREAM)

1 CUP BROWN SUGAR OR MORE TO TASTE

1. In a kettle, combine the chopped or ground fruit, raisins, and onion. Add the coarsely grated orange rind and the chopped fruit from between the membranes, the peeled and minced garlic clove, the spices, and horseradish. Stir in the water or juice starting with less and adding more as needed during the cooking.
2. Mix everything well and cook slowly, uncovered and stirring often, for about 1 hour or until thickened.
3. Add the sugar and continue cooking slowly to desired thickness, at least 10 minutes. Seal in sterile jars.

Yield: approximately 3 pints

ORANGE CHUTNEY

～◇◇◇◇～

This chutney is quite hot.

Ingredients:

3 NAVEL ORANGES

½ CUP CHOPPED DRIED APRICOTS

2 MEDIUM TART APPLES

1 SMALL ONION

1 MINCED HOT PEPPER OF CHOICE, OPTIONAL

¾ CUP RAISINS OR CURRANTS

1 CUP BROWN SUGAR

2 TABLESPOONS GINGER OR LESS TO TASTE

1 TEASPOON CLOVES

¼ TEASPOON CAYENNE PEPPER OR MORE TO TASTE

1 ½ CUPS CIDER VINEGAR, OR 1 CUP VINEGAR AND ½ CUP JUICE

1. Grate the oranges coarsely, remove the fruit from between membranes, and chop. Add the chopped dried apricots. Peel, core, and chop the apples. Peel and finely chop the onion. Add the raisins, brown sugar, ginger, cloves, pepper, and vinegar.

2. Mix everything well in a kettle and simmer gently until thick and soft, about 1 hour. Seal in sterile jars.

Yield: approximately 2 to 3 pints

*Note: Sugar and raisins can be added after cooking for a half hour, which will help avoid sticking. Stir often at the end of the cooking time.

INDIA APPLE CHUTNEY

～◇◇◇◇～

This chutney is quite hot.

Ingredients:

4 LARGE TART APPLES

2 LARGE YELLOW OR WHITE ONIONS

CHOPPED HOT PEPPER OF CHOICE, OPTIONAL

1 LB. PITTED DATES

2 CUPS VINEGAR

1 TEASPOON DRY MUSTARD
1 TEASPOON GINGER
1 TEASPOON ALLSPICE
¼ TO ½ TEASPOON CAYENNE PEPPER
FRUIT JUICE OR WATER AS NEEDED
2 CUPS BROWN SUGAR

1. Chop the peeled and cored apples, peeled onions, optional hot pepper, and pitted dates in a blender, food processor, or by hand. If you prefer a smoother sauce, these ingredients may be ground together.
2. Combine in a kettle with the vinegar, mustard, ginger, allspice, and cayenne pepper. Add the juice or water as needed to make a slightly runny mixture.
3. Cook until the fruits are soft, adding liquid as needed.
4. Add the brown sugar and cook slowly until thick and seal in sterile jars.

Yield: approximately 6 to 8 half-pint jars of chutney

KIWI CHUTNEY

This chutney is quite hot.

Ingredients:
12 KIWI FRUITS
1 LARGE ONION
2 LEMONS
1 CUP CHOPPED WHITE RAISINS
MINCED HOT PEPPER OF CHOICE, OPTIONAL
1 ½ CUPS VINEGAR, OR ½ CUP JUICE AND 1 CUP VINEGAR
1 CUP BROWN SUGAR
2 TABLESPOONS MINCED PRESERVED OR CANDIED GINGER OR MORE TO TASTE (YOU MAY
    ALSO USE GRATED PEELED FRESH GINGER BUT START WITH LESS AND ADD TO TASTE)
¼ TO ½ TEASPOON CAYENNE PEPPER

1. Coarsely grate the rind from the lemons and cut the fruit from membranes, discard seeds and chop the fruit saving any juice from the membranes.
2. Peel and chop the kiwi, onion, and raisins. Mix all ingredients well in a kettle and slowly cook, uncovered, for about 1 ½ hours. Stir often to break up pieces. When thick, seal in sterile jars.

Yield: approximately 2 pints

MISCELLANEOUS

SWEET FRUIT SAUCES, SYRUPS, AND RELISHES

APPLESAUCE

Ingredients:

RED COOKING APPLES, SUCH AS MCINTOSH IN WHATEVER AMOUNT YOU WISH

WATER

SUGAR

CINNAMON (OPTIONAL)

RED FOOD COLORING (OPTIONAL)

1. Wash, trim, cut up, and roughly core the apples. You do not need to remove the entire core since it will be removed when the sauce is strained. Put them into a kettle and add about ³/₄ cup water for each quart of cut-up apples or water about one-third of the way up the filled kettle. Bring to a boil and cook at a low boil until the apples are very soft stirring occasionally. Strain the apples, measure, and return to the kettle.
2. Add about ½ to ⅝ cup of sugar per quart of strained apples. If you like, you may also add 1 teaspoon of cinnamon per 4 quarts of the strained apples, or to taste. Adding a few drops of red food coloring will give the sauce a pleasantly rosy color.
3. Return slowly to a boil, stirring, and simmer for 10 minutes. Cook longer if too watery. Seal in sterile jars or freezer containers. A peck of apples, 8 quarts, will yield about 4 to 5 quarts of sauce and a bushel 20 to 25 quarts depending on how thick you want your sauce.

CINNAMON APPLES

Ingredients:
4 LARGE FIRM APPLES (CHOOSE A TYPE THAT WILL HOLD ITS SHAPE WHEN COOKED)
½ CUP WATER
½ CUP SUGAR
½ CUP LITTLE RED CINNAMON CANDIES (RED HOTS)

1. Wash, peel, and cut the apples into fairly thick wedges, about 6 per apple. Alternatively, cut crosswise into thick rounds and remove the cores.
2. In a straight-sided fry pan or large saucepan, make a syrup of the water, sugar, and cinnamon candies.
3. Simmer until the sugar and candies are dissolved, stirring constantly.
4. Add the apples, one layer at a time, and simmer until the apples are somewhat transparent but still holding shape. Cool on a plate and refrigerate.

Yield: approximately 24 apple slices

*Note: These slices are especially pretty served as a holiday salad when arranged in a flower shape on a lettuce leaf with a ball of cream cheese that has been rolled in chopped nuts in the center. The syrup left after cooking is a tasty addition to applesauce or served warm over desserts.

"LUMPY" APPLESAUCE

Ingredients:

APPLES (CHOOSE COOKING APPLES SUCH AS MCINTOSH IN ANY AMOUNT YOU WISH)

WATER

SUGAR

⅛ TO ¼ TEASPOON CINNAMON (OPTIONAL)

RED FOOD COLORING (OPTIONAL)

1. This applesauce does not get strained, so it will need a few extra preparation steps. Choose whatever type of apples you prefer, but ones that fall apart when cooked are preferable. To prepare the apples, peel, quarter, core, slice, and chop roughly. Place the apple chunks in a pan and keep underwater until all apples are prepared. This will help prevent browning.

2. When all apples are chopped, drain off the water until it only comes up the side of the pan about ⅓ the depth of the apples. Cook slowly until the apples are soft. If the chunks do not fall apart when they are very soft, mash with a potato masher or whir in a blender or food processor but leave small pieces for texture.

3. Measure the sauce and add ½ to ⅝ cup sugar per quart, taste before adding more. If you choose, you may add cinnamon and red food coloring for a rosy color.

4. Return the sauce to a simmer and cook, stirring often for 10 minutes and seal in sterile jars, freezer containers, or refrigerate once cool.

Yield: will be about the same as for strained applesauce

RUM RAISIN SAUCE

Ingredients:
1 cup sugar
⅓ cup water
2 cups dark raisins or currants
1 small orange
½ cup water
⅓ to ½ cup rum, preferably dark rum

1. Combine the sugar and water. Bring to a boil, stirring.
2. Wash the raisins or currants, picking over for any stems, and squeeze dry. Coarsely grate the orange rind and add along with the additional water to the mixture.

3. Simmer slowly for 15 minutes or more, covered, until quite thick, then cool to warm. And add the rum.
4. Store in a covered container at room temperature for several days. Use as a topping for ice cream, pudding, or cake and other desserts.

Yield: depends on how thick you make the sauce but it will be between 1 ½ to 2 cups

*Note: Variations can be made by using other dried, chopped fruits alone or with the raisins. Fruit-flavored liqueurs, such as peach brandy or orange liqueurs, can be used instead of the rum. The juice of the orange may be used instead of all or part of the water.

APPLE CATSUP

Ingredients:

4 LBS. FIRM APPLES, SUCH AS MCINTOSH

2 CUPS CIDER VINEGAR

3 CUPS SUGAR

1 TEASPOON WHOLE CLOVES

½ TEASPOON WHOLE ALLSPICE

½ TEASPOON PEPPERCORNS

1 CINNAMON STICK, BROKEN

2 TEASPOONS MUSTARD SEED

1. Make the apples into an unsweetened applesauce using as little water as possible. A microwave will help with this (see applesauce recipe, page 78).
2. Meanwhile, make a syrup by combining the remaining ingredients. If you prefer, the spices may be contained in a spice bag or tea caddy and removed when the sauce is done. Alternatively, you may substitute ground spices for the whole:

    ¼ teaspoon cloves

    ⅛ teaspoon allspice

    ⅛ teaspoon black pepper

    ¼ teaspoon dry mustard

    Your sauce will be darker and some experimentation may be needed.
3. Bring the syrup to a boil and simmer, tightly covered, for 30 minutes. For more flavor, make it the day ahead, simmer, and let stand overnight. Strain to remove the whole spices if left loose, and add the cooked strained apples.
4. Return to a simmer and cook for 20 to 30 minutes or until very thick. Stir often. A diffuser on the burner will be a big help.
5. Seal in sterile jars.

    Yield: will depend on the size of the apples and how thick the catsup—approximately 3 to 4 pints

LEMON CATSUP

⌐⌐⌐◦⌐◦⌐

This syrup is quite tart and spicy. Try it on seafood or chicken.

Ingredients:

12 MEDIUM, OR 10 LARGE, LEMONS

1 CUP SUGAR

1 TABLESPOON GRATED FRESH HORSERADISH (OR USE BOTTLED PURE HORSERADISH
    WITHOUT CREAM)

1 TABLESPOON POWDERED MUSTARD

1 TEASPOON TURMERIC

½ TEASPOON CLOVES

½ TEASPOON ALLSPICE

½ TEASPOON GROUND WHITE PEPPER

1 SMALL ONION, MINCED

A DASH OF CAYENNE PEPPER, OR MORE TO TASTE

1. Coarsely grate the rind from each lemon and juice all of them. Add sugar, horseradish, powdered mustard, turmeric, cloves, allspice, white pepper, finely minced onion, and cayenne pepper. Mix well and let stand, covered, overnight in a nonreactive container such as plastic, glass, or stainless steel.
2. The next day, bring to a boil and cook slowly, uncovered, for 30 minutes. Return to a tightly covered container and let stand for two weeks in a cool dark place, stirring daily.
3. Strain through a jelly bag, bring to a boil, and seal in sterile jars or refrigerate.

Yield: approximately 2 pints

*Note: This sauce is quite thin, so serving from a small bottle or with a spoon is a good idea. It would freeze well, perhaps as ice cubes, for using a little at a time.

APRICOT SAUCE

Ingredients:

11 OZ. DRIED APRICOTS

1 CUP DARK CORN SYRUP

1 CUP LIGHT CORN SYRUP OR BASIC SUGAR SYRUP (SEE BELOW)

½ CUP WATER

JUICE OF 1 LEMON OR ORANGE

1. Cook the dried apricots slowly, covered, in enough water to almost cover, until very tender and water is almost gone. Puree in a blender or food processor.
2. Transfer to a pan and add the dark corn syrup, light corn syrup (or basic sugar syrup), water, and juice.
3. Bring to a boil and simmer 10 to 15 minutes or until sauce as thick as you wish. Seal in sterile jars or refrigerate. This makes an excellent dessert or pancake topping.

Yield: approximately 2 to 3 pints depending on thickness

*Note: The same sauce can be made using 2 standard cans of apricots packed in as low sugar syrup as possible. Skip the first cooking, drain the apricots, and puree keeping the juices. Adjust the amount of sweetening added and mix in as much of the apricot juice as needed to make the texture you prefer. You will need to simmer the syrup for 10 minutes if it is to be sealed in sterile jars.

BASIC SUGAR SYRUP TO USE IN FRUIT SYRUPS

Ingredients:

2 ¼ CUPS SUGAR

2 ½ CUPS WATER

1. Dissolve the sugar in the water over low heat. Bring to a boil and cook to 220°F. Skim off any foam and store in the refrigerator tightly covered. Use within a week.

CRANBERRY SYRUP

Ingredients:
4 CUPS FRESH CRANBERRIES
2 ½ CUPS BASIC SYRUP (P. 84)
JUICE OF 1 LEMON
⅓ CUP RED PORT WINE (OPTIONAL)

1. Wash and pick over the cranberries. You may chop if desired. Add the basic syrup and lemon juice.
2. Cook at a slow boil for 10 minutes or until the cranberries are very soft. Cool and strain. For a clearer syrup, use a jelly bag. Add red port wine if desired. For additional flavor, let the cook fruit stand for several days before straining. Store in the refrigerator or seal in sterile jars.

Yield: will depend on how you strain the sauce and on how long it is cooked but there should be between 3 and 4 cups of syrup

*Note: All these fruit syrups will make attractive gifts in assorted small bottles.

LEMON SYRUP

Ingredients:
6 LEMONS
2 ½ CUPS BASIC SYRUP (P. 84)

1. Coarsely grate the lemon rinds, juice the lemons, and combine with the basic syrup in a pan.
2. Cook at a slow boil for 10 minutes, covered. It may be cooked longer, uncovered, to intensify the flavor. Let stand overnight, covered. Strain, reboil, and seal in sterile jars or refrigerate. When stored in the refrigerator, there is no need to reboil the syrup but it will boost the flavor.

Yield: determined by the size of your jars; it will be around 3 ½ to 4 cups of syrup, depending on the length of cooking.

LEMON ORANGE RUM SYRUP

Ingredients:

2 LARGE ORANGES

3 LEMONS

½ CUP DARK RUM

1. Make this syrup following the steps for the Lemon Syrup (p. 85).
2. Add the rum after straining. This syrup is best stored in the refrigerator, not sealed in jars.

Yield: around 1 ½ cups of syrup, depending on how long it has been cooked

CHOCOLATE SYRUP

Ingredients:

2 SQUARES UNSWEETENED COOKING CHOCOLATE

2 CUPS BASIC SYRUP (P. 84)

1 TABLESPOON BUTTER

1. Grate or chop the chocolate and combine with the syrup in the top of a double boiler. Heat over boiling water until chocolate is melted and mixture is smooth. Alternatively, heat in a microwave using medium power until smooth. Stir often and watch carefully.

2. Add the butter and mix well. Refrigerate and warm to serve over ice cream or other desserts.

Yield: around 2 cups of sauce

*Note: Be sure to use fresh chocolate. Older will not melt as well. Use additional chocolate if you like a stronger taste. For chocolate mocha sauce, add a bit of instant coffee to the warm sauce, and for a chocolate/mint sauce, add a little mint flavoring, which can be found in your grocery store where the vanilla is shelved.

POMEGRANATE SYRUP

Ingredients:
2 POMEGRANATES
JUICE OF 1 LEMON
2 CUPS BASIC SYRUP (P. 84)

1. Remove the seed sacks from the pomegranates and crush or whir in a blender or food processor. Strain the juice overnight using a fine mesh sieve or jelly bag.
2. Add the lemon juice and the basic syrup. Mix well, taste, and adjust the sweetness. For a sweeter sauce, add more of the basic syrup. Additional lemon juice will decrease the sweetness.

Yield: determined by how sweet or thick you make the syrup; uncooked syrup will give you around 3 cups

*Note: For thicker syrup, simmer the juices until quite thick and then add the syrup. Seal in sterile jars or refrigerate. For a refreshing drink, mix the syrup with soda water or a lemon/lime soda. You might prefer a less sweet syrup for use with a sweetened soda.

CINNAMON SYRUP

Ingredients:
4 CUPS FRESH APPLE JUICE (IF USING BOTTLED, MAKE SURE IT HAS AS LITTLE SUGAR AS POSSIBLE)
1 CUP BASIC SYRUP (P. 84)
½ CUP RED CINNAMON CANDIES (RED HOTS)
1 CINNAMON STICK, BROKEN
ADDITIONAL BASIC SYRUP OR LEMON JUICE FOR ADJUSTING SWEETNESS

1. Mix all ingredients except the additional syrup or lemon juice and simmer, uncovered, until fairly thick and syrupy.
2. Taste and adjust sweetness by adding additional syrup or a bit of lemon juice. Remove the cinnamon stick bits and seal in sterile jars or refrigerate for storage.

Yield: determined by how thick the syrup becomes; there will be around 3 to 4 cups of cinnamon syrup

*Note: For additional flavor, let the syrup stand for several days before straining.

GINGER SYRUP

Ingredients:

FRESH GINGER ROOT

1 LEMON

2 ½ CUPS BASIC SYRUP (P. 84)

1. Peel and finely chop or grate enough ginger root to measure 3 tablespoons. Coarsely grate the lemon rind and juice the lemon. Combine these with the basic syrup.
2. Simmer for 10 minutes, uncovered, and let stand overnight or longer. Strain and seal in sterile jars or refrigerate.

    Yield: approximately 2 ½ cups of ginger syrup

*Note: To seal these syrups, first return them slowly to a boil and then seal in hot jars. Pour into clean jars and cover to store in the refrigerator or pour into freezer containers and freeze.

UNCOOKED CRANBERRY RELISHES

For all these relishes, first wash and pick over the cranberries, discarding any soft berries. Then grind them or whir in a blender or food processor until they are as finely ground as you prefer. Mix all the ingredients well and store in the refrigerator. Powdered spices may be added for additional taste. Letting the relish age for a few days will improve and blend the flavors.

Recipe Number One

Ingredients:

4 CUPS CRANBERRIES

1 LEMON, RIND COARSELY GRATED AND FRUIT JUICED

1 CUP RAISINS, CHOPPED OR GROUND, OR USE WHOLE CURRANTS

2 CUPS SUGAR, ALL WHITE OR PART BROWN

Recipe Number Two

Ingredients:

2 CUPS CRANBERRIES

1 WHOLE ORANGE, WASHED AND GROUND, OR USE THE COARSELY GRATED RIND, RE-
MOVE THE PITH, AND CHOP OR GRIND THE FRUIT

1 CUP SUGAR, ALL WHITE OR PART BROWN

1 ½ CUPS MINIATURE MARSHMALLOWS

Recipe Number Three

Ingredients:

4 CUPS CRANBERRIES

1 LARGE ORANGE, GRIND OR USE JUST THE COARSELY GRATED RIND AND CHOPPED
FRUIT

3 LARGE SWEET APPLES, PEELED, CORED, AND EITHER GROUND, GRATED, OR FINELY
CHOPPED

3 CUPS SUGAR, ALL WHITE OR PART BROWN (TASTE FOR SWEETNESS AFTER 2 CUPS)

½ CUP COARSELY CHOPPED PECANS

STARTING
WITH CANNED FRUITS AND VEGETABLES

A wide variety of treats can easily be made in any season by starting with canned fruits and vegetables instead of fresh, so check your grocery store's supply and have fun.

PICKLED PEACHES

Ingredients:

2 STANDARD-SIZED CANS OF PEACHES IN LIGHT SYRUP (SLICES OR HALVES)

WATER

½ CUP CIDER VINEGAR

½ CUP SUGAR, WHITE OR BROWN

1 CINNAMON STICK, BROKEN

½ TEASPOON WHOLE CLOVES

½ TEASPOON WHOLE ALLSPICE

SEVERAL WHOLE CARDAMOM PODS (OPTIONAL)

1. Drain the peaches, set the fruit aside, and measure the juices. Add water to make 1 ½ cups of liquid. Pour it into a saucepan and add vinegar, sugar, and spices.
2. Bring the syrup to a boil and simmer, uncovered, for 10 minutes. Add the peaches and simmer 10 minutes more, uncovered.
3. Seal in sterile jars or refrigerate. Let it marinate several days before serving.

Yield: approximately 3 pints of pickles

*Note: Extra syrup can be boiled until thick and used as a dessert topping. It is especially good poured over pound cake.

PICKLED BEETS

Ingredients:

CANNED BEETS CUT AS YOU WISH (SEE THE DIRECTIONS FOR AMOUNT)

1 LARGE YELLOW ONION, PEELED AND SLICED INTO HALF-RINGS

2 CUPS BEET JUICE

½ CUP CIDER VINEGAR

¼ CUP SUGAR, WHITE OR BROWN

2 TEASPOONS WHOLE CLOVES

2 TEASPOONS MUSTARD SEED

2 TEASPOONS MUSTARD SEED

1 LARGE CINNAMON STICK, BROKEN

1. Drain and reserve the liquid from enough cans of beets, cut as desired, to make 2 quarts of beets. Set the beets aside and keep 2 cups of the juice for the syrup. Reserve the extra juice to use as needed.

2. Make a syrup of the 2 cups of juice, vinegar, and remaining ingredients.

3. Bring syrup to a boil and simmer, covered, for 15 minutes and add the peeled, sliced onion and beets.

4. Return to a boil and simmer, covered, for 10 minutes more. Seal in sterile jars or refrigerate. Let it age several days before serving. (The beets should be barely covered with syrup. If more is needed, add additional juice and vinegar.)

Yield: 5 pints with the onions, which may be omitted if you prefer

*Note: After the beets have been eaten, save the juice to make pickled eggs
(see p. 169).

LARGE-QUANTITY PICKLED PEACHES

Ingredients:

2 106-OZ. CANS PEACHES PACKED IN LIGHT SYRUP OR JUICE (HALVES OR SLICES)

2 LARGE CINNAMON STICKS, BROKEN

2 TEASPOONS WHOLE CLOVES

2 CUPS CIDER VINEGAR

8 WHOLE CARDAMOM PODS

WHOLE DRIED GINGER, BROKEN, TO TASTE

4 CUPS SUGAR

1. Drain the juice from the peaches and cook at a slow boil, uncovered, for 20 minutes along with the cinnamon, cloves, vinegar, cardamom, and ginger.
2. After 20 minutes, add the sugar and stir to dissolve. Add peaches and simmer for 10 minutes uncovered.
3. Seal in sterile jars.

Yield: 11 to 12 pints

*Note: If just a sweet spiced, not pickled, peach is preferred, replace the vinegar with more juice. If you like more spice flavor, add additional spices to taste.

LARGE-QUANTITY PICKLED BEETS

Ingredients:

8 15.25-OZ. CANS TINY WHOLE OR SLICED BEETS

3 CUPS BEET JUICE (FROM THE CANS)

3 CUPS CIDER VINEGAR

1 CUP WHITE SUGAR

1 TEASPOON WHOLE ALLSPICE

2 LARGE CINNAMON STICKS, BROKEN

2 TEASPOONS CRACKED DRIED GINGER

2 TO 3 ONIONS

1. Drain the beet juice from the cans and make a syrup with the juice, vinegar, sugar, allspice, cinnamon sticks, and whole cloves.
2. Cook the syrup at a slow boil for 20 minutes, uncovered.

3. Add the beets. Peel the onions, cut in half lengthwise, slice crosswise, and add to the mixture.
4. Return to a boil and simmer, uncovered, for 10 minutes.
5. Seal in sterile jars and let age at least a week before serving. Make sure that some of the spices go in each jar.

Yield: approximately 8 pints of pickles

*Note: Use the syrup left after eating these pickles to make pickled eggs (see p. 169).

FESTIVE FRUIT

Ingredients:
1 STANDARD CAN PEACHES, PACKED IN LIGHT SYRUP
1 STANDARD CAN PEARS, PACKED IN LIGHT SYRUP
1 STANDARD CAN APRICOTS, PACKED IN LIGHT SYRUP
1 LARGE CINNAMON STICK, BROKEN
2 TEASPOONS WHOLE CLOVES
1 PIECE DRIED GINGER ROOT, CRUSHED
1 TEASPOON WHOLE ALLSPICE
SEVERAL CARDAMOM PODS
½ TO ⅔ CUP BROWN SUGAR
⅓ CUP CIDER VINEGAR
1 6- TO 8-OZ. JAR RED MARASCHINO CHERRIES

1. Drain all juices from the fruits into a kettle and add the cinnamon stick, cloves, ginger root, allspice, and cardamom pods.
2. Boil rapidly until reduced to about 1 ½ cups and add the brown sugar (less for heavy syrup) and vinegar.
3. Simmer 5 minutes, covered. Add the fruits and the jar of red maraschino cherries, drained.
4. Simmer 5 minutes more and seal in sterile jars or refrigerate. Let it age for a week before serving. Makes a nice addition to a buffet table.

Yield: 3 to 4 pints

BRANDIED PEACHES

Ingredients:

CANNED PEACHES, PACKED IN HEAVY SYRUP, CUT AS YOU WISH

BRANDY

1. Start with any amount of canned peaches. Pour into a saucepan along with their juice and bring to a boil. Simmer 10 minutes. Pack peaches into sterile jars or refrigerator containers.
2. Fill each jar about ¾ full with the boiling syrup. Finish filling with brandy and seal. Let stand 3 to 4 weeks before serving.
3. Each standard can of fruit will give you about 1 ½ cups of finished fruit.

*Note: A few maraschino cherries in each jar will add a nice color. A slice of lemon per jar, simmered along with the fruit, will add extra flavor. Various fruit liqueurs or rum can be substituted for the brandy

If you prefer, some whole spices can be added to each jar. Consider stick cinnamon, whole cloves, or whole dried, cracked ginger. You may also start with fresh peaches. Remove skin and pits. Cut the peaches as you wish and simmer in a little water until almost tender but holding their shape. Drain and measure the juices. Add ¾ to 1 cup of sugar for every cup of juice. Heat until the sugar dissolves and then pour back over the peaches. Let stand for 30 minutes and continue with step 1 of the recipe. The number of peaches you use will determine your yield.

MINTED PEARS

Ingredients:

CANNED PEARS, PACKED IN HEAVY SYRUP

DRIED MINT

GREEN FOOD COLORING (OPTIONAL)

1. Start with any amount of canned pears, cut as you wish. Drain the syrup into a pan and add 1 teaspoon dried mint per can. Also a drop or two of green food coloring to add a nice color.
2. Simmer the syrup, covered, for 10 minutes and let steep, covered, for several hours or overnight.

3. Add the pears and simmer, covered, for 10 minutes.
4. Pack the hot pears into sterile jars and add boiling syrup to within ½ inch of the top and seal. Or pack in refrigerator containers and chill. Let it age at least two weeks for the flavor to soak into the pears.

Yield: each standard can of fruit will give you around a pint of finished pears

*Note: If you prefer to start with fresh pears, first cut them in half, pare, and remove cores. Cook in a little water along with the mint until almost tender but holding their shape. Green food color may be added to the water before the pears. Add sugar as in the Brandied Peach recipe (see p. 93) and then continue with step 4 of this recipe.

PICKLED CHERRIES

Ingredients:
CANNED SOUR CHERRIES, PACKED WITHOUT SUGAR
1 CUP CIDER VINEGAR
RED FOOD COLORING (OPTIONAL)
2 CUPS SUGAR

1. For each standard-sized can of sour cherries, drain very thoroughly in a strainer or colander and put into a glass bowl, jar, or other nonreactive container. Do not use aluminum. Discard the can juices.
2. Cover with the cider vinegar. Some red food color mixed into the vinegar will improve the color of the finished cherries.
3. Let stand, covered, at room temperature for 1 week. Shake gently or stir each day.
4. At the end of the week, drain the cherries very well. Add the sugar to the liquid and bring to a boil to dissolve, stirring. Pour back over the cherries while hot. Let stand for 4 days, stirring each day.
5. Drain off the juice, bring to a boil, and pour back over the fruit. Let stand 4 more days. They are now ready to serve as a dessert topping or with meats.
6. To seal the cherries in sterile jars, bring the fruit to a boil in the juice and then pour into jars and seal.

*Note: There are no spices in this recipe. If you wish, in step 1, add whole spices of your choice. If you are processing several cans of cherries at once, you may not need all the sugar per can. Additional sugar can be added when the syrup is boiled in step 5, if needed.

BRANDIED CHERRIES
FOR CHERRIES FLAMBÉ

Ingredients:

1 STANDARD CAN SWEET CHERRIES

¼ CUP COGNAC OR GOOD BRANDY

2 TABLESPOONS KIRSCH, ORANGE LIQUEUR, OR OTHER FRUIT LIQUEUR

½ TEASPOON CINNAMON

¼ TEASPOON CLOVES

ADDITIONAL BRANDY FOR FLAMING

1. Drain the cherries well. Discard the juice and combine the cherries with the rest of the ingredients.
2. Cover and refrigerate for several days before using, stirring daily.
3. Before serving, heat in a chafing dish or pan until just barely simmering; do not boil. Warm 1 tablespoon cognac in a metal ladle, ignite with a match, and pour over the cherries. When the flame has died, serve the cherries over ice cream or other dessert. A chafing dish will make a classic presentation. Be sure to dim the lights before flaming.

Yield: approximately 4 servings

SWEET AND SOUR SAUCE

Ingredients:

9 OR 10 OZ. JAR PLUM JAM

9 OR 10 OZ JAR. APRICOT JAM

9 OR 10 OZ JAR ORANGE MARMALADE

½ CUP CIDER VINEGAR (FOR A MILDER SAUCE, USE ⅓ CUP)

1 TEASPOON GINGER

½ TEASPOON CLOVES

1. Combine all ingredients. Heat slowly to a boil, stirring, and simmer for 5 minutes. Store in the refrigerator. To seal in sterile jars, first simmer for 10 minutes.

Yield: approximately 2 pints

*Note: This sauce is very tasty served with dishes such as chicken and pork or with stir-fry and other Asian-inspired dishes.

PEACH CATSUP

This catsup is somewhat spicy.

Ingredients:
28 OZ. CAN SLICED PEACHES IN MEDIUM OR HEAVY SYRUP
1 SMALL TO MEDIUM ONION
FINELY GRATED RIND AND FRUIT OF 1 ORANGE OR 1 LEMON
½ CUP VINEGAR
½ TEASPOON CLOVES
½ TEASPOON ALLSPICE
½ TEASPOON GINGER
SEVERAL DROPS HOT SAUCE TO TASTE
BROWN SUGAR AS NEEDED

1. Drain and chop the peaches. Retain the juice. Peel and chop the onion. Puree the peaches, onion, lemon fruit, and grated peel together in a blender or food processor. If necessary, a little of the vinegar may be added to make processing easier.
2. Put the peach juice in a pan and boil down to about ½ cup. Combine the fruit, juice, vinegar, spices, ginger, and hot sauce.
3. Cook slowly until it begins to thicken, stirring often. Taste for sweetness, and if desired, add brown sugar, ¼ cup at a time to taste. Continue cooking, stirring often, until a nice thick sauce appears.

Yield: approximately 1 pint depending on thickness

*Note: For a spicier sauce, add more hot sauce or some minced hot pepper before pureeing. To start with fresh peaches, peel and pit enough to measure about 3 cups of diced peaches. Puree as in step 1 of the recipe and continue making the catsup. You will need to add sugar and may need to add some water to replace the canned syrup.

ITALIAN OLIVES

Ingredients:

32 oz. jar Spanish olives, drained and liquid retained (if whole, cut an X on each end; if stuffed, remove the pimento, chop, and add it to the sauce)

½ cup finely chopped celery

¼ cup finely chopped green and/or red sweet pepper

1 large garlic clove, finely minced

1 small yellow onion, finely chopped

1 tablespoon finely chopped parsley

1 teaspoon mixed Italian herbs (p. 191) or more to taste

⅓ cup vegetable oil

⅓ cup cider, white wine, or red wine vinegar

⅓ cup liquid from olives

4 drops hot sauce

fresh ground pepper to taste

1. Combine all ingredients in a bowl. Cover and let stand at room temperature all day, mixing several times. Pour into a nonreactive container.
2. Store in the refrigerator and let age for 2 to 3 weeks for better flavor. If liquid does not cover the olives, add more oil, vinegar, and olive liquid in equal amounts. You will probably be able to return the mixture to the olive jar or a widemouthed quart jar. Serve with a slotted spoon and eat the seasonings along with the olives.

*Note: When olives have been eaten, the remaining liquid will make a tasty addition to many salad dressings.

OLIVE TAPENADE

Ingredients:

5 ½ oz. jar Manzanilla olives stuffed with pimiento, or a rounded cup of your favorite olives

1 tablespoon very finely chopped onion and garlic, combined in whatever proportions you wish

2 teaspoons white wine vinegar or vinegar of choice

2 teaspoons olive oil of choice (vegetable oil will also work)

1 scant teaspoon Dijon mustard or prepared mustard of choice

½ teaspoon Worcestershire sauce

3 drops hot sauce

1. Finely chop the olives. This is best done by hand as it is easier to control the texture.
2. Combine all the ingredients and mix well.
3. Store several days in the refrigerator to blend the flavors before serving as a cracker spread.

Yield: approximately ¾ cup

CHILI SAUCE

Ingredients:

2 QTS. CANNED CRUSHED TOMATOES WITHOUT SEASONING EXCEPT SALT

2 MEDIUM YELLOW ONIONS

1 SMALL GREEN PEPPER

1 CUP CIDER VINEGAR

JUICE OF ½ LEMON

½ TO 1 CUP SUGAR (FOR A LESS SWEET SAUCE, START WITH ½ CUP)

1 ½ TEASPOONS DRY MUSTARD

1 TEASPOON CLOVES

1 TEASPOON CHILI POWDER OR TO TASTE

1. Wash, cut up, and finely chop the onions and green pepper. For a smoother sauce, use a blender or food processor.

2. Combine all ingredients and slowly bring to a boil. Cook slowly until desired thickness, stirring often. Scrape the bottom of the kettle very well. As the sauce thickens, it will tend to stick. When thick, seal in sterile jars. You will have between 3 and 4 pints of sauce depending on how thick you make it.

*Note: When the sauce has cooked for a while, chill a spoonful and taste for salt. Add some if needed, but most canned tomato products usually will have enough.

PRIVATE BLEND SALSA

This recipe is intended as a framework that you can use to develop your own salsa blend. If you prefer a smooth salsa, puree the mixture in a blender or food processor before cooking.

Ingredients:

14.5 OZ CAN PETITE CHOPPED TOMATOES (DISCARD ANY GREEN OR CORE PIECES)

¼ TO ⅓ CUP FINELY CHOPPED GREEN SWEET PEPPER

⅓ CUP MINCED YELLOW ONION

2 GARLIC CLOVES, MINCED

MINCED HOT PEPPER (SEE NOTE BELOW)

1 to 2 tablespoons sugar

2 tablespoons lime juice, bottled or fresh

1 tablespoon cider vinegar

½ teaspoon salt (or to taste if tomatoes are unsalted)

4 shakes hot sauce

1 teaspoon minced fresh parsley

⅛ teaspoon cilantro

⅛ teaspoon leaf oregano

⅛ teaspoon ground cumin

⅛ teaspoon ground coriander

⅛ teaspoon thyme

1. Combine all ingredients in a saucepan. Mix well and simmer, uncovered, for 30 minutes, stirring occasionally.

2. At this point, your salsa may be sealed in sterile jars or stored in the refrigerator for immediate use when chilled.

Yield: approximately 1 ½ cups

*Notes: Hot peppers vary considerably in their amount of heat. One medium jalapeno will give a nicely spiced mild salsa. For fierier salsa, experiment with habanera or Serrano peppers. Handle the peppers carefully using gloves to protect your hands and try to avoid breathing the steam from the bubbling pan, especially when using hotter peppers. See page 157 for notes on the relative heat of different peppers. After trying this recipe, you can easily branch out and develop your own special salsa. Other ingredients such as fruits are often used, and altering the amount of these ingredients will alter the final product, so let your imagination go and create for yourself.

SPICY HOT SAUCE

Commercially made hot sauces are best left to the companies that have made them for years but it is possible to make a very good sauce of your own at home. The amount of heat you prefer in your sauce is easily controlled and the use of your sauce is open to your imagination.

Ingredients:

8 oz. can tomato sauce

3 habanera peppers, roughly chopped

1 Serrano pepper, chopped

1 small yellow onion, chopped

1 or 2 cloves garlic, chopped

2 tablespoon cider vinegar

1 teaspoon sugar

¼ teaspoon leaf thyme

¼ teaspoon paprika

¼ teaspoon ground coriander

¼ teaspoon leaf cilantro

¼ teaspoon black pepper corns, rounded, or ¼ to ½ teaspoon freshly ground black pepper

1. Combine all ingredients in a blender or food processor. Process until pureed and transfer to a small lidded saucepan. Put over low heat. A diffuser is best for this sauce. Simmer at a low bubble for 30 minutes, keeping the lid ajar. This sauce will spit if a lid is not used, but you want steam to escape.

2. When the sauce is thick enough for your use, cool and transfer to a glass jar for refrigerator storage. It may also be sealed in sterile jars or frozen for future use.

Yield: approximately 1 cup

*Note: The sauce will give a boost to soups, stews, salad dressings, and anywhere you want some heat, but add it in small amounts and taste as you go. When hot, it will taste hotter than when chilled, so use care.

The number and type of peppers you use will determine the heat for your finished sauce. See page 157 for a listing of the relative heat found in different peppers. This number of peppers will give an extremely hot sauce, so you may wish start with fewer since habanera peppers are one of the hottest peppers that are easily available unless you grow your own.

Remember to use care when working with hot peppers. Protect your hands with gloves when cutting them. Always avoid breathing over any container they are cooking in, and if you use a garbage disposal for the trimmings, use it with cold water and do not get your head above while it is running. It is always a good idea to be prepared for nose blowing at any time and keep your hands from touching your face. Hot pepper in the eyes is not pleasant.

ITALIAN TOMATO SAUCE

Ingredients:

2 48-oz. cans tomato juice (for a chunkier sauce, replace 1 can with an equal amount of crushed tomatoes)

28 oz. can tomato puree, or 2 small cans tomato paste

3 to 4 cloves garlic

1 carrot

1 medium onion

½ green sweet pepper

½ cup minced celery

3 tablespoons lemon juice

3 tablespoons minced parsley

3 to 4 tablespoons mixed Italian herbs (p. 191)

1 tablespoon sugar

fresh ground black pepper to taste

¼ to ½ cup dry red wine (optional)

1. Crush or mince the garlic, finely shred the carrots, and mince the onion and pepper. Combine all ingredients in a large kettle and simmer until desired thickness. Taste for salt when partly cooked and add if needed.

2. You will have about 3 ½ quarts of sauce when using the tomato puree. Seal in sterile jars in sizes that you will be using at one time.

*Note: For a smooth sauce, puree the vegetables in a blender or food processor with some of the tomato juice. Serve the sauce on pizza, with meat on pasta, or in dishes that call for a basic Italian tomato sauce.

SEAFOOD COCKTAIL SAUCE

Ingredients:

6 OZ. CAN TOMATO PASTE

1 TABLESPOON MINCED ONION

1 TABLESPOON MINCED GREEN SWEET PEPPER

1 TABLESPOON MINCED CELERY

2 TO 4 TABLESPOONS GRATED FRESH OR PREPARED HORSERADISH (WITHOUT CREAM)

3 TABLESPOONS FRESH LEMON JUICE

½ TEASPOON HOT SAUCE, OR TO TASTE

½ TEASPOON SALT

1. Combine all ingredients and mix well. Refrigerate in a nonreactive container. The sauce will often thicken in the refrigerator, so just stir well before serving.

Yield: a generous cup

BARBECUE SAUCE

Ingredients:

16 oz. can crushed tomatoes

1 small onion, minced

1 clove garlic, minced or crushed

2 tablespoons brown sugar, or more to taste

½ cup catsup or part chili sauce

½ cup cider vinegar

¼ cup Worcestershire sauce

1 teaspoon salt or to taste

1 teaspoon dry mustard

¼ teaspoon cloves

dash of cayenne pepper or to taste

liquid smoke (optional)

1. Combine all ingredients, mix well, and simmer until desired thickness, stirring often. Store in a glass jar in the refrigerator. Ingredients may be multiplied for a larger batch of sauce and sealed in sterile jars.

   Yield: approximately 1 to 1 ½ pints

TOMATO GARLIC CATSUP

Ingredients:

20 oz. can pureed tomatoes

½ cup sugar

several cloves fresh garlic, minced

juice of 1 lemon

½ teaspoon salt

½ teaspoon ginger

¼ teaspoon dry mustard

1. Combine all ingredients and simmer until desire thickness, about 1 hour. Taste the catsup as it cooks and add more seasonings, sugar, or salt if it is needed for your taste.

   Yield: approximately 1 pint depending on thickness

*Note: This recipe does not include onion, but some could be added, minced finely.

*Variation: Reduce the garlic and puree some green pepper and onion along with the garlic and some of the tomatoes before cooking.

PICKLED
VEGETABLES

Many of the winter season's crisp vegetables will pickle very nicely. There is always a good supply available at supermarkets and greengrocers. In summer, visit your own garden or local farmer's market for the freshest vegetables. Be sure to select really crisp, fresh vegetables and use them as soon as possible. Most of these pickles will need time in salt or brine to remove excess water so that the pickling solution can take its place, so plan accordingly.

DILLED BEANS

Ingredients:

2 LBS. SLIM, STRAIGHT, FRESH GREEN OR YELLOW BEANS, OR A COMBINATION

½ CUP COARSE SALT

2 QTS. WATER

2 ½ CUPS WHITE OR CIDER VINEGAR

2 ½ CUPS WATER

1 TABLESPOON COARSE SALT

1 TABLESPOON MIXED PICKLING SPICES (P. 192)

½ TEASPOON GARLIC POWDER, OR 2 CLOVES FRESH GARLIC, CRUSHED

1 TABLESPOON DILL SEED

1 TEASPOON MUSTARD SEED

¼ TEASPOON CRUSHED DRY CHILIES, OR ½ TEASPOON BLACK PEPPER CORNS

1 LARGE GARLIC CLOVE (PEELED AND CUT IN HALF IF A STRONGER GARLIC FLAVOR IS
    DESIRED)

1. Wash the beans very carefully and remove ends and any blemishes. Make a brine of ½ cup coarse salt dissolved in 2 quarts cold water and soak the beans for 3 to 4 hours, or overnight, in a cool place. Drain well and rinse several times. Let soak in freshwater for 30 minutes and drain again.
2. Mix together the vinegar, water, salt, pickling spices, and garlic powder. Simmer, covered, for 10 minutes. For added flavor, do this when the beans go into the brine and let steep longer.
3. Pack beans upright in sterile pint jars, leaving at least ¾ inch headroom. Some beans may need to be trimmed to fit. Add some dill seed, mustard seed, chilies, and a slice of garlic clove, if using, to each jar.
4. Reboil the syrup and pour into the jars leaving ½ inch headroom. Wipe the rims carefully and attach a sterilized lid and rim. Screw on tightly and process 15 minutes in boiling water (see p. 8). These are low, acid foods, so they need this processing for safe storage. Refrigerated beans will not need this processing if they are to be used in a few days.

Yield: 3 to 4 pints

*Note: Experiment with the spices to reach your desired degree of heat and taste.

DILLED CAULIFLOWER

Follow the Dilled Beans recipe (p. 106), substituting cauliflower broken into flowerets for the beans. Buy about 2 lbs. or 1 large head.

DILLED MIXTURES

Combine firm crisp vegetables of your choice and follow the recipe for Dilled Beans (p. 106). For example: Pack the bottom half of the jar with evenly trimmed green beans and the top with broken cauliflower, or a layer of carrot slices or short sticks. Other combinations could include carrot sticks, small whole onions, green or red pepper strips, and celery. For even cooking, vegetables should all be cut about the same size where possible. If quart jars are used, you will need to process them for 20 minutes in the hot water.

SPICY CABBAGE

Ingredients:

4 QTS. SHREDDED CABBAGE

½ CUP COARSE SALT

Syrup ingredients for every quart of salted cabbage:

2 CUPS CIDER VINEGAR, OR VINEGAR OF CHOICE

½ TO 1 CUP SUGAR, DEPENDING ON DESIRED SWEETNESS

1 TABLESPOON MUSTARD SEED

1 TABLESPOON PREPARED HORSERADISH, WITHOUT CREAM

1 TEASPOON WHOLE CLOVES

4 CINNAMON STICKS, BROKEN

1 TEASPOON CRUSHED, DRY RED CHILIES

1. In a nonreactive container, mix the shredded cabbage well with the coarse salt. Let stand, covered, overnight at room temperature.

2. Rinse in a colander and press out excess water. Measure the cabbage. For every quart of measured cabbage, make a syrup of 2 cups cider vinegar. Add the sugar, mustard seed, horseradish, cloves, cinnamon, and red chilies. Combine and simmer, covered, for 15 minutes. Let the syrup stand for at least 30 minutes. There will be more flavor if the syrup is allowed to steep overnight. After steeping, it may be strained for a clear syrup.

3. Pack the cabbage loosely into sterile jars, reboil the syrup and fill the jars to ½ inch of the top.

4. Seal and process for 20 minutes in boiling water.

Yield: 4 to 5 pints

*Note: If you use the cabbage within a few days, it does not need to be processed. The cabbage could be served hot as a side dish or cold as a salad.

PICKLED CAULIFLOWER

Ingredients:

1 LARGE HEAD CAULIFLOWER

3 LARGE YELLOW OR WHITE ONIONS

¼ CUP COARSE SALT

¾ CUP CIDER OR WHITE VINEGAR

¾ CUP WATER

¼ TO ½ CUP SUGAR, DEPENDING ON DESIRED SWEETNESS

1 TEASPOON MUSTARD SEED

½ TEASPOON WHOLE CLOVES

½ TEASPOON TURMERIC

½ TEASPOON CELERY SEED

¼ TEASPOON CRUSHED, DRY CHILIES, OR MORE TO TASTE

1. Break the cauliflower into pieces and wash. Drain well. Peel, quarter, and slice the onions crosswise. Mix the vegetables with the salt and let stand, covered, overnight. Drain well and rinse thoroughly. Let stand in cold water for 30 minutes and drain thoroughly again.

2. Combine the vinegar, water, sugar, mustard seed, cloves, turmeric, celery seed, and chilies and simmer for 10 minutes, covered. Let steep overnight for added flavor.

3. Add the vegetables and boil until tender-crisp, about 5 to 10 minutes. Seal in sterile jars covered with syrup.

Yield: approximately 3 pint jars

*Note: Extra syrup will be good in salad dressing.

PICKLED FRESH MUSHROOMS

Ingredients:

1 lb. button mushrooms

salt

½ cup canola or corn oil

¼ to ⅓ cup cider vinegar (may be part lemon juice, if desired)

½ cup finely chopped celery, finely chopped

4 tablespoons chopped salad olives with pimento

¼ to ⅓ cup finely chopped red onion, to taste

1 tablespoon Worcestershire sauce

1 tablespoon minced parsley

1 clove garlic, minced or crushed

½ teaspoon salt

fresh ground black pepper, to taste

minced green sweet or hot pepper (optional)

crushed dry red chilies (optional)

1. Wash and trim the mushrooms. Leave whole if small or cut in half, or quarters if large. Cook for 10 minutes in 1 inch of water and 1 teaspoon salt. Drain well.

2. Gently mix the hot mushrooms with a dressing made by combining the rest of the ingredients. Pour into a quart jar and refrigerate for several days before enjoying.

*Note: The jar will not be full to the top. If you wish, more mushrooms may be cooked, but the jar will not hold another whole pound. It will not be necessary to increase the syrup, but if needed, a little more vinegar can be added.

MINTED ONION RINGS

Ingredients:

MEDIUM WHITE ONIONS (SEE THE PROCESSING DIRECTIONS FOR THE AMOUNT NEEDED)

2 CUPS WHITE OR CIDER VINEGAR

2 TABLESPOONS WHITE SUGAR

2 TABLESPOONS DRIED MINT LEAVES

1 TABLESPOON COARSE SALT

5 CUPS WHITE ONION RINGS

GREEN FOOD COLORING

1. Simmer the vinegar, sugar, mint leaves, and salt together, covered, for 10 minutes. Remove from the heat and let stand while you prepare the onions. There will be more flavor if the syrup steeps overnight.

2. Process enough medium-sized white onions to make 5 cups lightly packed onion rings. Peel the onions and slice them crosswise about ⅜-inch thick. Save the ends for another use and separate the slices into rings. If using large onions, cut in half lengthwise before slicing into half rings. Strain the syrup, if you wish, and add several drops of green food coloring for a brighter appearance.

3. Combine the onion rings and syrup. Heat to boiling, cook 1 minute, and pack in sterile jars.

Yield: approximately 2 pints

GOLDEN ONION SLICES

Ingredients:

1 TABLESPOON DRY MUSTARD

1 TABLESPOON COARSE SALT

2 TEASPOONS TURMERIC, OR 1 EACH OF TURMERIC AND CURRY POWDER

1 ½ TEASPOONS BLACK PEPPERCORNS, OR ½ TEASPOON CRUSHED DRY RED CHILIES

1 TEASPOON MUSTARD SEED

¼ TEASPOON CLOVES

¼ TEASPOON GINGER

2 CUPS CIDER VINEGAR

2 TABLESPOONS SUGAR (OPTIONAL—IF YOU WANT A SLIGHTLY SWEETER SYRUP)

2 LARGE BERMUDA ONIONS

1. Make a syrup by mixing the mustard, salt, turmeric, peppercorns, mustard seed, cloves, ginger, and vinegar (and sugar, if you are using). Simmer together, covered, for 10 minutes, then set aside to steep while preparing the onions. For added flavor, let steep overnight.

2. Peel the onions, cut in quarters, and slice about ¼-inch thick crosswise. White or Vidalia onions may also be used alone or as a mix. If the onions are smaller, only cut them in half lengthwise before slicing. Place the onions in a large flat kettle. This will help avoid overcooking due to the bottom layers getting hot before the top. If this is not possible, cook the onions in batches since overcooking will give you a soft pickle.

3. Add boiling water to cover and quickly bring just to a boil. Drain in a colander. If the slices are to be sealed, pack them loosely in sterile jars while still hot. Return the syrup to a boil, and pour over the pickles. You may need more vinegar for all the jars, so be sure some of the spices are in each jar and add boiling vinegar as needed.

4. For refrigerator storage, reheat the syrup, add the onions, and let stand at room temperature for several hours before putting into clean jars and covering. Allow to age several days.

Yield: approximately 3 pints depending on the size of the onions

PICKLED WHOLE MINI ONIONS

Ingredients:

20 OZ. BAG FROZEN TINY WHITE PEELED ONIONS OR 4 CUPS FRESH PICKLING ONIONS

½ CUP COARSE SALT

WATER

2 CUPS WHITE OR WHITE WINE VINEGAR

½ CUP WHITE SUGAR

1 TABLESPOON MIXED PICKLING SPICES

½ TEASPOON PREPARED HORSERADISH, WITHOUT CREAM

¼ TEASPOON CRUSHED CHILIES

1. Thaw the frozen onions in cold water and drain well. If using fresh small white pickling onions, immerse them in boiling water for 2 minutes, drain, and chill in cold water. The peel should easily slip off.

2. Make a brine of the salt dissolved in enough water to cover the onions. Add the onions and let stand overnight with a plate on top, weighted down with a water-filled jar. On the next day, drain and rinse the onions well in freshwater.

3. Combine the vinegar, sugar, pickling spices, horseradish, and chilies, and simmer 10 minutes, covered, or let steep overnight for added flavor.

4. Bring the syrup to a boil, remove from the heat, and add the onions. Let stand for 3 minutes to warm the onions. Pack them in sterile jars, reboil the syrup, and pour over the onions, being sure that some of the spices are in each jar. Seal the jars. For refrigerator storage, let the onions cool in the syrup and pour in to storage jars.

Yield: 2 pints

*Note: Frozen onions will produce a softer pickle. For crisp pickles, fresh must be used. For added flavor, add to each jar one sliced garlic clove, a small bay leaf, and additional chilies. If any syrup is left over, try it, strained, in salad dressing.

PICKLED BANANA PEPPERS

Ingredients:

BANANA PEPPERS (ENOUGH TO FILL 2 PINT JARS)

2 CUPS CIDER VINEGAR

½ CUP WATER

¼ CUP SUGAR

1 TEASPOON MIXED PICKLING SPICES (P. 192)

1 TEASPOON WHOLE BLACK PEPPERCORNS, OR A DRY CHILI PEPPER

1 TEASPOON MUSTARD SEED

2 GARLIC CLOVES

1 TEASPOON PREPARED HORSERADISH, WITHOUT CREAM

2 SMALL BAY LEAVES

1. Wash enough banana peppers to fill 2 pint jars, leaving a little space for spices. Leave the peppers whole, or if large, cut in half and remove stems and seeds.
2. Combine the vinegar, water, and sugar, and bring to a boil.
3. Fill each pint-sized jar with peppers and add half of the pickling spices, whole black peppercorns, mustard seed, garlic clove (peeled and cut in half), horseradish, and bay leaf.
4. Pour the boiling syrup over the peppers and allow to cool before storing in the refrigerator. Without a hot water processing, which will soften the peppers, it is best to not to seal these pickles for storage.

*Note: Other types of peppers, either alone or as a mixture, can also be pickled using this recipe. A slice or two of onion will give a different taste to this recipe as well.

PICKLED PEPPERS

Ingredients:

PEPPERS OF ANY TYPE (ENOUGH TO PACK INTO ONE QUART-SIZED JAR)

BAY LEAF, BROKEN

DRIED CHILI PEPPERS

ONION, SLICED

PEPPERCORNS

WHOLE CLOVES

MUSTARD SEED

CORIANDER SEED

CRUSHED WHOLE DRIED GINGER

1 ½ CUPS CIDER VINEGAR

⅓ CUP SUGAR

1 TEASPOON COARSE SALT

1. Wash the peppers, remove stems and cores and cut into large pieces and pack loosely into one sterile quart-sized jar or two pints. Use green or red sweet peppers, yellow banana peppers, hot green peppers, or other types that are available. Select only one type or use a mixture of peppers.
2. Evenly distribute among the peppers, in the desired amounts, the bay leaf, chili peppers, onion, peppercorns, cloves, mustard seed, coriander seed, and dried ginger.
3. Make a syrup by mixing the vinegar, sugar, and salt. Simmer together, covered, for 10 minutes.
4. Cover the peppers with the hot syrup, let cool, and store in the refrigerator for at least 2 weeks before serving. A month is even better.

STUFFED PICKLED PEPPERS

Ingredients:

6 SMALL SWEET PEPPERS, GREEN OR RED SWEET

½ CUP COARSE SALT

WATER

Seasoning ingredients:

3 CUPS CIDER VINEGAR

1 CUP WATER

3 TABLESPOONS SUGAR

1 TEASPOON CELERY SEED

1 SMALL CINNAMON STICK, BROKEN

1 TEASPOON MUSTARD SEED

1 TEASPOON PREPARED HORSERADISH, WITHOUT CREAM

1 TEASPOON WHOLE CLOVES

1 TEASPOON BROKEN DRIED GINGER ROOT

1 TEASPOON BLACK PEPPERCORNS

Filling ingredients:

3 CUPS FINELY SHREDDED WHITE CABBAGE

1 TEASPOON SALT

¼ CUP MINCED CELERY

1 MEDIUM CARROT, SHREDDED

1 CLOVE GARLIC, MINCED

2 TABLESPOONS SUGAR

1 TABLESPOON MUSTARD SEED

2 TEASPOONS PREPARED HORSERADISH, WITHOUT CREAM

1. Wash the peppers, remove and set aside the tops, remove the seeds, but leave the peppers whole. Soak the peppers and their tops overnight in a brine of the salt dissolved in enough water to cover. Weigh everything down with a plate topped with a water-filled jar.

2. On day 1, also make a spiced vinegar by simmering together vinegar, water, sugar, celery seed, cinnamon, mustard seed, horseradish, ginger root, and peppercorns, for 10 minutes, covered. Set the vinegar aside to steep overnight, covered. The next day, drain and thoroughly rinse the peppers and their tops. Put to dry upside down on a rack or towel.

In a bowl, mix together the shredded cabbage and salt. Let stand for 1 hour, rinse well, and drain very well. Add the celery, carrot, garlic, sugar, mustard seed, and horseradish to the cabbage and mix well. Use to stuff the peppers. Do not pack tightly. Tie the tops on with string.

3. Strain the vinegar, if you wish, and bring to a boil while packing the peppers into two clean, hot quart jars.

4. Slowly pour the vinegar over the peppers, and cover the jars. If you do not strain the vinegar, make sure some of the seasonings are in each jar. This will add flavor. Let cool and store in the refrigerator for several weeks before serving as a cold side dish or heat, but do not boil, in the syrup and serve hot.

Yield: approximately 2 quart jars

*Note: If more vinegar is needed, add plain boiling cider vinegar. Any extra spiced vinegar will make good salad dressing. One of the spiced vinegars starting on p. 185 can be used instead of making the spiced vinegar included in this recipe. Any leftover filling would be a nice addition to a salad.

ZUCCHINI SLICES

For each quart of finished pickles, you will need the following ingredients:

3 ZUCCHINIS (ABOUT ½ LB.)

1 MEDIUM WHITE OR YELLOW ONION

2 TABLESPOONS COARSE SALT

1 CUP CIDER VINEGAR

½ CUP WHITE SUGAR

1 TEASPOON MUSTARD SEEDS

½ TEASPOON CLOVES

½ TEASPOON TURMERIC (OPTIONAL)

1 CLOVE GARLIC, MINCED, OR ¼ GARLIC POWDER (OPTIONAL)

1. Slice the zucchini very thinly into enough crosswise slices to measure 1 quart. Thinly slice the onion. Combine the vegetables and mix with salt. Let stand 1 hour and rinse. Drain well and press out the water. The vegetables will have shrunk enough in volume to allow for the bulk of the onion in each quart.
2. Combine the remaining ingredients and simmer for 10 minutes, covered, or let steep while the vegetables are in the brine. Reheat for the next step.
3. Remove syrup from the heat, add the vegetables, and let stand for 1 hour, covered.
4. Pack in 1 hot sterile quart jar or 2 pints, cover with boiling syrup, and store in the refrigerator.

FRESH VEGETABLE PICKLE

~⚬∽∾⚬∾⚬∾

This is a nice addition to a snack table.

Prepare the vegetables in any amount, using just one type or a mixture, of the following:

CARROTS, CUT INTO LONG, SLIM STICKS

CELERY, CUT INTO LONG, THIN STICKS

CAULIFLOWER, BROKEN INTO FLORETS

SMALL, SLENDER SALAD ONIONS, LEAVE ON SOME OF THE GREEN TOP (IF LARGE, THEY
      MAY BE CUT LENGTHWISE IN HALF OR QUARTER)

SMALL WHITE PICKLING ONIONS, PEELED

CUCUMBER, CUT TO MATCH THE OTHER VEGETABLES

Other ingredients for each quart of prepared vegetables:

1 CUP CIDER VINEGAR

2 CUPS WATER

1 CUP WHITE SUGAR

1 TABLESPOON MUSTARD SEED

1 TEASPOON SALT, OR TO TASTE

⅛ TEASPOON GARLIC POWDER

¼ TEASPOON ONION POWDER

SEVERAL DROPS HOT SAUCE OR CRUSHED RED CHILIES TO TASTE (OPTIONAL)

1. Pack the veggies into whatever size jar you wish, trimming to fit. Do not overpack. The jars should be clean and hot to avoid breaking when the syrup is added.
2. Combine the vinegar, water, sugar, mustard seed, and salt (add hot sauce or chilies now if using) and simmer, covered, for 10 minutes. The syrup may steep overnight for added flavor. Reheat for the next step.
3. Pour the boiling syrup and spices over the vegetables, being sure some spices are in each jar. Cool to room temperature, and store in the refrigerator. Let age for a week before serving. After enjoying the vegetables, the strained syrup can be used in salad dressing.

WINTER MIXTURE

~~~~~

Prepare 5 quarts of cut vegetables (use only one type if desired, but a mixture is better). Choose from:

CUCUMBER

CELERY

CABBAGE

CAULIFLOWER

HOT PEPPERS

RED AND GREEN SWEET PEPPERS

YELLOW OR WHITE ONIONS

CARROTS, SLICED OR IN STICKS

BANANA PEPPERS

HOT PEPPERS

Brine ingredients:

¾ CUP COARSE SALT

3 QUARTS WATER

Syrup ingredients:

3 ¼ CUPS VINEGAR

3 ¼ CUPS WATER

1 CUP SUGAR

JUICE OF 1 LEMON

3 TABLESPOONS MIXED PICKLING SPICES (P. 192)

HOT PEPPER SAUCE OR CRUSHED RED CHILIES (OPTIONAL)

GARLIC CLOVES, MINCED (OPTIONAL)

1. Cut the chosen vegetables into bite-sized pieces trying to get them all about the same size. Make a brine by dissolving the salt in the water. Add the vegetables, cover, and soak overnight, weighted down.
2. Combine the syrup ingredients and simmer, covered, for 15 minutes. Remove from the heat and let steep overnight.
3. On day 2, reheat the syrup and add the vegetables. Let stand for 4 hours, covered.
4. Reheat to almost a boil and quickly pack the hot vegetables in sterile jars. Top with boiling syrup and seal. Be sure to include some of the seasonings in each jar.

    Yield: approximately 4 quarts

    *Optional: Add to each jar 1 bay leaf; 1 large garlic clove, sliced; and 1 dry chili, crushed.

SHREDDED SWEET PICKLES

❦

Ingredients:

6 CUPS MIXED, COARSELY SHREDDED FIRM VEGETABLES, SUCH AS CUCUMBERS,
    CABBAGE, ONIONS, AND CARROTS
¼ CUP COARSE SALT
1 QUART WATER

Syrup ingredients:

1 ½ CUPS WHITE SUGAR
1 ½ CUPS CIDER VINEGAR
1 ½ CUPS WATER
2 TABLESPOONS MUSTARD SEED
¼ CUP PICKLING SPICES (P. 192)

1. Prepare the shredded vegetables. Make a brine of the salt dissolved in the water. Add the vegetables and soak for 4 hours, covered. Drain in a colander and rinse well. Squeeze out as much water as possible.

2. Combine the sugar, vinegar, water, mustard seed, and pickling spices, and simmer together, covered, for 15 minutes. This can be done when the vegetables are set to brine. The extra steeping time will add to the flavor.

3. Reheat the syrup. Add 2 cups of the vegetables to the hot syrup, bring just to a boil, and quickly pack the shreds into a hot sterile pint jar. Top with boiling syrup and seal. Repeat with the rest of the vegetable shreds.

Yield: approximately 2 to 2 ½ pints

*Note: Your favorite whole pickling spices may be used instead of the mixed spices.

JANUARY WATERMELON RIND PICKLES

Ingredients:

10 LBS. SEEDLESS WATERMELON

½ CUP COARSE SALT

2 QUARTS COLD WATER

Syrup ingredients:

3 CUPS WHITE SUGAR

2 CUPS COLD WATER

2 CUPS CIDER VINEGAR

1 LARGE CINNAMON STICK, BROKEN

1 TEASPOON WHOLE CLOVES

1 TEASPOON WHOLE ALLSPICE

1 TEASPOON CRACKED DRY GINGER ROOT

1 LEMON

1. Cut the watermelon in half crosswise and then each half into two or three pieces lengthwise. Cut each piece into 1 inch slices crosswise. Remove the red flesh and keep for another use (see watermelon jelly and sorbet on pp. 39-40) or enjoy as fresh fruit.
2. Lay each slice on its side, cut off just the thin dark green rind with a sharp knife, and cut the light green rind into 1 inch chunks.
3. Make a brine by dissolving the salt in the cold water. Put the chunks in a large pan and pour on the brine. Weigh down the chunks with a plate topped with a water-filled jar so that all chunks are submerged in the brine. Let soak overnight at room temperature.
4. The next day, drain and rinse well under running water in a colander. Redrain and return to the pan. Cover the chunks with fresh cold water and simmer for about 1 hour until tender. Drain well in the colander.
5. Make a syrup of the sugar, cold water, vinegar, cinnamon, cloves, allspice, and ginger root. Simmer for 10 minutes, covered. Add the rind chunks and the lemon, cut in half lengthwise and thinly sliced crosswise. Discard seeds and thick ends.
6. Cook at a simmer, uncovered, for about 1 hour until the chunks appear translucent.
7. Pack the pickles in hot sterile jars, top with syrup, and seal. Make sure some of the spices and lemon are in each jar. Let the pickles age 1 week before enjoying.

Yield: 5 to 6 pints

*Note: The syrup can be made the night before and let stand, covered until needed. To make these pickles in summer, choose melon with as thick a rind as possible and follow the recipe. You will want to purchase about 10 pounds of melon. Any extra syrup can be refrigerated to use in another batch of pickles.

SALAD BAR PICKLES

～✦～

Visit your grocery store's salad bar and select a variety of firm vegetables or purchase them in the produce department. At home, cut so that the pieces are all about the same size. You will need about 5 cups of cut-up vegetables, such as:

CARROTS

CAULIFLOWER

CELERY

CUCUMBER

ONION

SWEET PEPPERS

If some heat is wanted, add a jalapeno pepper. A good variety will make a more colorful pickle.

Brine ingredients:

¼ CUP COARSE SALT

1 QUART COLD WATER

Syrup ingredients:

1 CUP WATER

1 CUP CIDER VINEGAR

⅓ TO ½ CUP SUGAR

½ TEASPOON CRACKED DRY GINGER

½ TEASPOON WHOLE CLOVES

½ TEASPOON WHOLE ALLSPICE

½ TEASPOON MUSTARD SEED

1 CINNAMON STICK, BROKEN

¼ TEASPOON TURMERIC

CRUSHED DRY CHILIES

DRY MINCED GARLIC OR ONION

CELERY, DILL SEED, OR DILL WEED

½ TEASPOON MUSTARD POWDER

1. Mix the vegetables in a nonreactive bowl. Make a brine by dissolving the salt in the cold water and pour over the vegetables. Cover and let stand overnight or about 12 to 14 hours. Drain, rinse well with freshwater, and drain thoroughly again. Taste for saltiness, and if too salty, soak in freshwater for 1 hour or more.

2. At the same time, make the syrup by combining water, vinegar, sugar, spices, cinnamon, turmeric, chilies, garlic or onion, celery or dill seed, and mustard powder in a saucepan. Simmer, covered, for 10 minutes and let steep overnight.

3. Return the syrup to a boil and add the drained vegetables and return to a rolling boil. Pack the pickles in sterile jars, top with boiling syrup being sure that some of the spices are in each jar, and seal. Store in a cool, dry place for several weeks before serving.

Yield: 2 pints

*Note: You may strain the syrup before using. However, leaving the spices with the pickles adds flavor as they age.

PICKLED CARROTS

When the Salad Bar Pickles (pp. 124-125) are sealed, if there is at least ½ cup syrup left, consider making this recipe.

Ingredients:
SMALL CARROTS
1 TEASPOON SALT
1 CUP WATER
SYRUP FROM SALAD BAR PICKLES RECIPE (pp. 124–125)
MINCED DRY GARLIC, ONION POWDER, MUSTARD SEED, HOT SAUCE (OPTIONAL)

1. Cut enough small carrots into quarters lengthwise to fill a half-pint jar. Make a brine of the salt and water in a nonreactive bowl, and soak the carrots for 1 hour. Rinse and drain well.
2. Heat the syrup, adding some of the additional seasonings if desired.
3. Add the carrots, bring to a boil, and store in the refrigerator in a half-pint jar or other nonreactive container. Let them age at least 1 week before serving. This is a nice addition to a veggie plate or salad.

Yield: 1 half-pint jar

COCKTAIL CARROTS

Ingredients:

CARROT STICKS

½ CUP CIDER VINEGAR

½ CUP WATER

1 TO 4 TABLESPOONS SUGAR

⅛ TEASPOON SALT (TASTE A CARROT AFTER BRINING TO DECIDE IF MORE SALT IS
    NEEDED)

SEASONING OF CHOICE (GARLIC, ONION, DILL SEED, MUSTARD SEED, CARAWAY SEED,
    AND/OR HOT SAUCE)

1. Fill 2 clean half-pint jars with thin carrot sticks, cut to fit.
2. Make a syrup of vinegar, water, sugar, salt, and seasoning(s) of choice.
3. Bring to a boil and pour over the carrots. Cover and let age in the refrigerator for 5 to 7 days before serving. Use within two weeks.

Yield: 2 half-pint jars of pickles

*Note: Small white boiling onions, celery sticks, or slices of cucumber can be processed the same way.

PICKLED MATCHSTICKS

Ingredients:

¾ CUP CIDER VINEGAR

¾ CUP WATER

1 CINNAMON STICK, BROKEN

½ TEASPOON WHOLE CLOVES

½ TEASPOON ALLSPICE

½ TEASPOON CRACKED DRY GINGER

1 LONG ENGLISH CUCUMBER

1 SMALL TO MEDIUM YELLOW OR WHITE ONION

1 TABLESPOON SALT

⅓ TO ½ CUP SUGAR OR TO TASTE

1 TEASPOON MUSTARD SEED

1. The night before making the pickles, prepare the syrup. In a saucepan, combine the vinegar, water, cinnamon, and spices. Simmer, covered, for 15 minutes. Leave covered and let stand overnight.

2. The next day, prepare the vegetables. Peel the cucumber, cut lengthwise into quarters, and remove any mature seeds. Cut the quarters crosswise into 3 equal sticks. Cut each stick lengthwise into thin slices and then cut the slices into matchsticks. Peel the onion, cut lengthwise in half, and slice crosswise into thin slices. Separate into half rings.

3. Mix the vegetables in a nonreactive bowl and mix in the salt. Let stand for 1 hour at room temperature. Drain, rinse well, and press out the water.

4. Strain the syrup and add the sugar and mustard seed. Simmer until the sugar is dissolved, stirring, and bring to a boil. Add the vegetables and return just to a boil. Quickly transfer the vegetables to a hot sterile jar with a slotted spoon. Reboil the syrup and pour over the pickles to fill the jar. Seal and store in a cool dark place for at least 1 week or up to 1 month before serving. The pickles may be stored in the refrigerator unsealed but flavor will develop more slowly that way.

Yield: approximately 1 ½ pints

*Note: Flavor variations are easy to create by altering the amount of sugar, adding other spices such as crushed chili peppers, or adding other vegetables such as sweet peppers cut into matchsticks. If you prefer, all the spices may be left in the syrup. In that case, add the mustard seed to the syrup when it is made. A variation on this recipe follows below:

MATCHSTICK DILLS

Syrup ingredients:

¾ CUP WATER

¾ CUP VINEGAR

¼ TO ½ TEASPOON CRUSHED RED CHILIES

1 TEASPOON DILL SEED

1 SMALL GARLIC CLOVE, PEELED AND SMASHED

2 TO 3 TABLESPOONS SUGAR (ADDED TO THE DRAINED SYRUP; DILL PICKLES ARE NOT AS SWEET)

1. Make the syrup with these ingredients and the pickles as in the above recipe.

HOT CONFETTI MATCHSTICKS

Follow the directions for Pickled Matchsticks (p. 128) using these ingredients for the syrup and vegetables.

For the syrup:

¾ CUP CIDER VINEGAR

¾ CUP WATER

1 TEASPOON CRUSHED RED CHILIES, OR MORE TO TASTE

SEVERAL DROPS HOT SAUCE

½ TEASPOON BLACK PEPPERCORNS

¼ TEASPOON MINCED DRY GARLIC, OR ONE SMASHED FRESH GARLIC CLOVE

¼ TEASPOON WHOLE CLOVES

¼ TEASPOON CRACKED DRY GINGER

Remaining ingredients:

4 CUPS ASSORTED MATCHSTICK-CUT VEGETABLES

1 TABLESPOON SALT

3 TO 4 TABLESPOONS SUGAR

1 TEASPOON MUSTARD SEEDS

1. Make a syrup using the vinegar, water, chilies, peppercorns, garlic, cloves, and ginger.
2. Prepare an assortment of matchstick-cut vegetables to loosely measure about 4 cups. A selection to start with is ½ volume of cucumber, ½ volume of carrots, onion, or sweet peppers (red peppers keep their color best).
3. Brine in salt for 1 ½ hours. The longer time is for the denser vegetables.

4. Add to the strained syrup the sugar and mustard seeds. Follow the matchstick instructions and seal in sterile jars.

Yield: approximately 3 half-pint jars

*Note: For a hotter pickle, consider adding 1 shredded jalapeno pepper.

CUCUMBER PICKLES

Cucumber pickles can be made year-round, and quite acceptable pickles can be made in the winter if a few extra steps are taken. Cucumbers sold in winter are usually coated with wax to retard spoilage, so they must be peeled. Also, the seeds need to be removed since they tend to be hard in mature cucumbers and pickling syrups will make them harder. Don't expect the color of your winter pickles to be the same as summer pickles, with no rind to add the expected green color and ripe cucumbers are a lighter color than young summer pickling cucumbers. But do expect the flavor to be tasty, the texture to be crisp, and the processing easy. Be sure to let your pickles age a few weeks to develop flavor. If you have access to long English or burp-less cucumbers that usually come sealed in plastic, use them in these recipes. They usually have tender enough skins so that peeling is not necessary and the seeds do not tend to get hard.

CUCUMBER ONION PICKLE CHUNKS

Ingredients:

2 LARGE SLIM WINTER CUCUMBERS OR 1 ENGLISH CUCUMBER

1 LARGE WHITE OR YELLOW ONION

2 TABLESPOONS COARSE SALT

¾ CUP CIDER VINEGAR

¼ CUP WATER

¼ CUP SUGAR

1 TEASPOON MIXED PICKLING SPICES (P. 192)

1. Peel the cucumbers quarter lengthwise, remove the obvious seeds, and cut into chunks. If using an English cucumber, it is not necessary to peel first. Peel the onion, cut into quarters, and slice fairly thin, crosswise. Combine in a large bowl. Sprinkle the vegetables with the salt, mix, and let stand overnight.

2. The next day, rinse thoroughly and drain completely, or spread on a towel. Combine the vinegar, water, sugar, and pickling spices, and simmer, covered, for 10 minutes.

3. This can be done at the same time as the vegetables are processed and allowed to steep overnight at room temperature. Return the syrup to a boil, add the vegetables, and bring just to a boil. Quickly pack into sterile jars, cover with boiling syrup and seal. These pickles may be stored, unsealed, in the refrigerator, but let them age for a few weeks before enjoying.

Yield: 1 to 2 pints, depending on the size of your vegetables

*Note: Work quickly when the pickles boil since overcooking will result in soft pickles.

MIXED PICKLES

Follow the recipe for Cucumber Onion Pickle Chunks (p. 132), but substitute some of the ingredient for these.

Ingredients:

ASSORTED VEGETABLES (CAULIFLOWER, CARROT SLICES, GREEN OR RED SWEET
    PEPPERS)
ONIONS
1 TEASPOON TURMERIC (OPTIONAL)

1. Add vegetable pieces cut about the same size as the cucumber chunks. These should equal the amount of the cucumber chunks in the recipe on p. 132 for a balanced mixture. Tiny whole onions can be used in place of the sliced onions.
2. Double the syrup ingredients in the recipe and follow the given steps to complete the recipe. Add turmeric, if desired, to add a golden glow to your pickles.

Yield: approximately 1 ½ quarts

*Note: For a taste variety, add several garlic cloves, peeled and quartered if large. For a hotter pickle, add several drops of hot pepper sauce or use cayenne pepper.

UKRAINIAN FRESH CUCUMBER PICKLES

These pickles can be made at any time of the year and in any amount, but since they are not heated, they cannot be sealed in jars. They should be eaten within a week or two and always stored in the refrigerator.

Ingredients:

LONG, SLIM ENGLISH CUCUMBERS

WHITE OR YELLOW ONIONS

SALT

WATER

CIDER VINEGAR

SUGAR

MUSTARD SEED

GARLIC POWDER

BLACK PEPPERCORNS

¼ TO ½ TEASPOON MINCED DILL WEED, PREFERABLY FRESH

1. Slice as much cucumber as you wish into about 1/8 inch slices. Peel the onion and cut in half lengthwise. Slice crosswise as much as you wish into slices about the same thickness as the cucumber. Place these into a nonreactive bowl and measure how much water is needed to cover completely. Drain off the water and make a brine of the same amount by dissolving pickling salt in water at the ratio of 1 teaspoon salt per 1 cup of water. Stir to dissolve and pour over the vegetables. Refrigerate, covered, for 12 hours or overnight.
2. Make the pickling syrup at the same time. Start with about ½ the volume of water used in the brine, and for every cup, add ⅓ cup cider vinegar (more or less to taste), 1 or 2 tablespoons sugar, 2 teaspoons mustard seed, ⅛ teaspoon garlic powder, and 1 teaspoon black pepper corns.
3. Bring the pan to a boil, cover, and let simmer very slowly for 10 minutes, covered. Set aside at room temperature to steep overnight.
4. The next morning, drain the vegetables, rinse well, and drain thoroughly again. Place back in the bowl or in a glass or plastic jar. Add the minced dill weed. Pour on the pickling solution, being careful to include all the seasonings, and refrigerate at least 12 hours before serving.

*Note: For a quart of pickles, you will need one whole English cucumber, one medium onion, and a pickling solution made of:

1 ½ CUPS WATER

3 TABLESPOONS SUGAR

¼ TEASPOON GARLIC POWDER

½ CUP CIDER VINEGAR

2 TO 3 TEASPOONS MUSTARD SEED

1 TEASPOON BLACK PEPPER CORNS

¼ TO ½ TEASPOON DILL WEED (FOR THE JAR)

1. If more pickling solution is needed, add a spoonful more water and vinegar. If a hot pickle is wanted, add several drops hot sauce or a chopped hot pepper. The amount of sugar and dill are easily altered to suit your taste, so some experimentation may be needed. Minced fresh garlic may be substituted for the powder. It will give a stronger taste. To make a mixed fresh pickle, include other vegetables of choice, such as carrots, celery, and cauliflower.

BREAD AND BUTTER PICKLES

Ingredients:

1 LONG, FIRM ENGLISH CUCUMBER (IF AVAILABLE, USE 1 ½ LBS. PICKLING CUCUMBERS
    INSTEAD)

1 MEDIUM YELLOW OR WHITE ONION

2 TABLESPOONS COARSE SALT

2 CUPS CRACKED ICE

Syrup ingredients:

¾ CUP WHITE SUGAR

1 ¼ CUPS CIDER VINEGAR

¼ CUP WATER

A PINCH OF RED PEPPER OR SEVERAL DROPS HOT SAUCE

½ TEASPOON DRY MUSTARD

½ TEASPOON TURMERIC

½ TEASPOON GARLIC POWDER

½ TEASPOON CELERY SEED (OPTIONAL)

1. Wash the cucumber and slice about ¼ inch thick. Peel the onion, cut in half lengthwise, and slice crosswise into half circles about the same thickness as the cucumbers. Mix the vegetables in a bowl and toss with the salt and cracked ice. Let stand for 3 hours.
2. Combine the syrup ingredients in a pan. Bring the syrup to a boil and simmer for 5 minutes, covered. Let steep while the vegetables are on ice. Rinse and drain the vegetables well. Return the syrup to a boil.
3. Add the vegetables and bring back to a boil, stirring often. Boil for 1 minute, stirring.
4. Quickly pack the vegetables into hot sterile jars, cover with boiling syrup, and seal. Let them age 1 week before serving.

Yield: approximately 3 pints, depending on the size and type of the cucumbers used

WINTER PICKLES

Ingredients:
1 LONG ENGLISH CUCUMBER OR 2 LONG, SLENDER SUMMER CUCUMBERS

Brine ingredients:
3 TABLESPOONS COARSE SALT
1 ½ CUPS WATER

Syrup ingredients:
1 CUP CIDER VINEGAR
½ CUP WATER
½ CUP WHITE SUGAR
1 TABLESPOON MUSTARD SEED
1 TABLESPOON MIXED PICKLING SPICES (CAN BE TIED IN A BAG)
A FEW DROPS HOT SAUCE (OPTIONAL)

1. Peel the summer cucumbers, no need to peel English cucumbers. Then quarter length-wise, remove any obvious seeds, and cut into chunks. In a bowl, soak overnight in brine made of the salt dissolved in the water. Place a small plate on top of the cucumbers and weigh it down with a clean jar filled with water. The cucumbers must be completely submerged. On the next day, rinse the cucumbers thoroughly and drain well.

2. Combine the syrup ingredients in a saucepan large enough to also hold the cucumbers. Simmer, covered, for 10 minutes. If the syrup is made when the cucumbers go into the brine and allowed to steep overnight, there will be more flavor. The mixed spices may be left loose in the syrup.

3. Add the cucumbers and bring just to a boil. Quickly pack hot in sterile jars, cover with boiling syrup, and seal. Or pack in a quart jar, add the spice bag and syrup, and store in the refrigerator.

Yield: approximately 2 pints

*Note: These pickles are only slightly sour. For a truly sour pickle, reduce the sugar to ¼ cup. For a sweeter pickle, let them stand overnight in the syrup. Next day, drain and add ¼ cup sugar to the syrup. Bring to a boil and pour back over the pickles. Let them stand for a few minutes to warm, pack the chunks into jars, top with boiling syrup, and seal. For an even sweeter pickle, repeat the addition of ¼ cup sugar at one-day intervals before sealing. Sugar must be added slowly to cucumbers to preserve their texture.

ICY TIME DILLS

Ingredients:

1 LONG, SLIM ENGLISH CUCUMBER OR 2 SLIM CUCUMBERS

3 TABLESPOONS COARSE SALT

Syrup ingredients:

1 CUP CIDER OR WHITE VINEGAR

1 CUP WATER

3 TABLESPOONS SUGAR

2 TABLESPOONS COARSE SALT

1 TABLESPOON DILL SEED, OR TO TASTE (IF FRESH DILL WEED IS AVAILABLE, WASH
AND ADD SOME TO THE JAR WHEN PACKING)

½ TEASPOON CRUSHED CHILIES, OR ⅛ TEASPOON CAYENNE PEPPER

¼ TEASPOON GARLIC POWDER, OR 1 OR 2 GARLIC CLOVES, MINCED

1 LARGE BAY LEAF, BROKEN

1. Peel the cucumbers, if not using English cucumber, quarter lengthwise, remove seeds, and cut into chunks. Toss lightly with the salt and let stand overnight. Rinse and drain well.
2. Combine the vinegar, water, sugar, salt, dill seed, chilies, garlic powder, and bay leaf, and simmer, covered, for 15 minutes. Let steep overnight.
3. Return the syrup to a boil, add the cucumbers, and bring back just to a boil. Seal in sterile jars, adding some fresh dill weed sprigs to each jar, if using. If using more than one jar, be sure to distribute the spices equally. Cover the pickles with boiling syrup and seal. Let them age before serving.

Yield: approximately 1 quart

*Note: If the pickles are all put into one jar, the spices can be tied in a bag for cooking and then go into the jar with them for flavor or just leave the spices loose in the jar.

DARK CHUNKS

Ingredients:

4 LARGE, SLIM CUCUMBERS (OR 2 ENGLISH CUCUMBERS)

3 TABLESPOONS COARSE SALT

Syrup ingredients:

1 CUP CIDER VINEGAR

¼ CUP WATER

⅔ CUP BROWN SUGAR

2 TEASPOONS WHOLE CLOVES

1 LARGE CINNAMON STICK, BROKEN

1 SMALL PIECE DRIED GINGER ROOT, BROKEN

1. Peel the cucumbers, quarter, remove seeds, and cut into chunks (if using English cucumbers, wash, cut in quarters lengthwise, and cut into chunks). Add the salt, mix well, and let stand overnight. Rinse and drain well.
2. Combine all the syrup ingredients and simmer, covered, for 10 minutes. Leave the syrup to steep overnight.
3. Return the syrup to a boil. Add the cucumbers, heat just to a boil, quickly pack pickles into hot sterile jars, cover with boiling syrup, and seal or store in the refrigerator. Let them age at least a week before enjoying.

Yield: 2 to 3 pints

SWEET CHUNKS

Ingredients:
4 LARGE, SLIM CUCUMBERS (OR 2 ENGLISH CUCUMBERS)
½ CUP COARSE SALT
1 QUART WATER

Syrup ingredients:
1 CUP CIDER VINEGAR
½ CUP SUGAR
⅓ CUP WATER
JUICE OF 1 LEMON
2 TABLESPOONS MIXED PICKLING SPICES (OR 1 CINNAMON STICK, BROKEN, 1 TEASPOON
 WHOLE CLOVES, ½ TEASPOON WHOLE ALLSPICE, AND 1 TEASPOON DRIED GINGER
 ROOT, BROKEN)

1. **Day 1**: Prepare the cucumbers by peeling, quartering, removing any large seeds, and cutting into chunks (if using English cucumbers, wash, cut in quarters lengthwise, and cut into chunks).
2. In a bowl or large pan, make a brine by dissolving the salt in the water. Add the cucumbers and weigh them down under the brine with a plate held down by a water-filled jar. Let stand in a cool place, not a refrigerator, for 3 days.
3. **Day 4**: Drain off the brine, rinse the cucumbers, and cover with cold water. Let stand for another 3 days. Drain well.
4. **Day 7**: Combine the syrup ingredients, stir well, bring to a boil, and simmer, covered, for 10 minutes.
5. Add the cucumbers and bring just to a boil. Remove from the heat and leave at room temperature for 1 day.
6. **Day 8**: Drain off the syrup, add ¼ cup sugar, bring to a boil, and pour back over the pickles. Leave for another day.
7. **Day 9**: Add another ¼ cup sugar as before. If the pickles are to be sealed in jars, wait a few minutes for them to warm, pack in hot sterile jars, cover with boiling syrup, and seal. If to be stored in the refrigerator, let the pickles cool in the syrup and pack in clean jars, top with syrup, and cover the jars. Let the pickles age for a week before serving.

Yield: 3 to 4 pints

*Note: If more brine or syrup is needed, make more in the same proportions. The pickles will shrink during the salting and the sweetening steps, so don't be worried by a little lack of liquid at the beginning of each step.

RELISH

Many relishes can easily be made in winter or in summer and fall since they are tradition-ally made from the types of firm vegetables that store well. Green tomatoes are one exception. These are found in many relishes and they can be ground and frozen before frost ends the fresh tomato season. Or if you have a friendly produce department at your grocery store, green tomatoes can also be obtained during winter months. Today, tomatoes are often shipped from warm climates while still green to help avoid bruising and spoilage. They are then allowed to ripen before going out for sale. A friendly greengrocer or produce department manager is well worth cultivating for this purpose.

After trying some of these relish recipes, you might wish to develop your own signature relish blend. Most any of the hard crisp vegetables that are sold in winter (or grown in summer) can be successfully ground or chopped into relishes. Several frozen vegetables will work also.

Some of the vegetables you might like to consider are:

- Cabbage
- Carrots
- Cauliflower
- Celery
- Corn, frozen or fresh
- Cucumbers
- Garlic
- Green and red sweet peppers
- Green and ripe tomatoes
- Green and yellow beans
- Hot peppers
- Onion

- Radish
- Turnip
- Zucchini

Fruits can also be used in relishes and many are available fresh and frozen, so experiment with them as well.

The only extra equipment you will need to make relish is a grinder. Blenders and food processors can be used but it is very hard to control the texture with them and you do not want a pureed relish. A hand-cranked grinder that clamps on the edge of a counter or table will work the best, but always protect the surface with a cloth between the table or counter and the grinder. If you own a stand mixer, investing in the grinder attachment will be a handy addition to your kitchen equipment. When grinding a variety of vegetables, it works better to first mix the chopped vegetables and not to try to grind only one type at a time.

Relishes should be cooked in a heavy-bottom pan and stirred often, especially after any sugar is added. They easily stick as they get thicker and you don't want a runny relish, so a long cooking time is often necessary.

If you want a little extra zip to your relish, feel free to grind some hot peppers along with the other vegetable in any recipe or add hot sauce to the syrup mixture.

GREEN TOMATO RELISH

Ingredients:

2 QTS. CUT-UP GREEN TOMATOES

¼ CUP COARSE SALT

¼ MEDIUM CABBAGE

2 GREEN SWEET PEPPERS

1 RED SWEET PEPPER

1 HOT PEPPER (OPTIONAL)

GARLIC CLOVES (OPTIONAL)

1 CUP CIDER VINEGAR (MORE MAY BE NECESSARY)

2 CUPS SUGAR

2 TEASPOONS CELERY SEEDS (OPTIONAL)

2 TEASPOONS MUSTARD SEED

½ TEASPOON GROUND CLOVES

¼ TEASPOON GROUND ALLSPICE

GARLIC POWDER, OR GRIND A PEELED GARLIC CLOVE WITH THE VEGETABLES (OPTIONAL)

1. **Day 1**: Grind the tomatoes, add the salt, and leave to drain overnight in a cloth bag or large strainer. This is necessary due to the high water content in tomatoes, which would make your relish runny.
2. **Day 2**: Grind the cabbage and peppers, drain well, and in a kettle, combine with the drained tomatoes. Add vinegar starting with 1 cup and adding more as necessary during cooking. Stir in the remaining ingredients. Juices from the ground cabbage and vegetables can also be used for liquid during cooking.
3. Cook at a simmer until the vegetables are tender and the liquid is well reduced.
4. Seal in sterile jars.

Yield: 3 to 4 pints depending on how thick you want your relish

PEPPER RELISH

Ingredients:

4 RED SWEET PEPPERS

4 GREEN SWEET PEPPERS

3 LARGER (OR 2 JUMBO) YELLOW ONIONS

1 LARGE CUCUMBER

1 HOT PEPPER (OPTIONAL)

FRESH GARLIC TO TASTE (OPTIONAL)

2 MCINTOSH APPLES

2 CUPS CIDER VINEGAR

1 ½ TABLESPOONS MUSTARD SEED

2 TEASPOONS COARSE SALT

1 TEASPOON PREPARED HORSERADISH, OR MORE TO TASTE

½ TEASPOON CLOVES

½ TEASPOON CINNAMON

GARLIC POWDER TO TASTE OR GRIND FRESH GARLIC WITH THE OTHER VEGETABLES
(OPTIONAL)

1 TO 2 CUPS SUGAR

1. Wash the peppers, remove the stems and seeds, and cut into small chunks. Peel the onions and cut into small chunks. Remove the rind from the cucumber, cut into quarters lengthwise, remove any noticeable seeds, and cut into small chunks. If you choose to add hot peppers, cut up along with the sweet peppers. Including some of the seeds will increase the heat. Fresh garlic may also be ground with the vegetables.

2. Mix the vegetables together and grind using a hand or powered grinder. Drain off the juices, which can be saved for flavoring soups and stews later or added to the relish as it cooks if more liquid is needed. A good storage method is to freeze the juice in ice cube trays and then store in an airtight bag in the freezer.

3. Put the ground vegetables into a large pot and cover with boiling water. Let stand for 5 minutes and drain well in a large sieve.

4. Return the vegetables to the pot. Peel, core, and chop the apples. Grind them, saving the juices. Add the apples and juice to the pot. Stir in the remaining ingredients and mix well. Bring the kettle to a boil, reduce heat, and simmer until the vegetables are tender. It may be necessary to add water or additional vinegar, ½ cup at a time, if the vegetables become too dry and start to stick to the bottom. Taste the relish to decide if you want it tarter before adding vinegar. Some of the vegetable juices left from grinding may also be used.

5. Add sugar—2 cups will give a sweet relish; 1 cup will give a somewhat sweet relish. It is a good idea to start with less sugar and add more slowly to get the sweetness you want. Remember that the hot relish will taste sweeter than the chilled.

6. Return the kettle to a boil and simmer at least 10 minutes before sealing in sterile jars.

Yield: approximately 6 pints

*Note: The recipe can easily be halved for a smaller yield.

THREE CS RELISH

Ingredients:

2 CUPS FINELY SHREDDED CABBAGE

2 TEASPOONS SALT

1 CUP COARSELY SHREDDED CARROT

1 CUP FROZEN CORN, THAWED OR USE FRESH CORN CUT FROM THE COB

¾ CUP CIDER VINEGAR

½ CUP SUGAR

¼ CUP WATER

1 TEASPOON DRY MUSTARD

½ TEASPOON CELERY SEED (OPTIONAL)

½ TEASPOON MUSTARD SEED

1. Add the salt to the finely shredded cabbage and let stand 1 hour. Rinse and drain well.

2. In a small pan, simmer the shredded carrots and corn for 2 minutes in a little water and drain. Mix all the vegetables together in a bowl.

3. Combine the remaining ingredients in a pan large enough to hold the vegetables and simmer, covered, for 10 minutes.

4. Add the vegetables, bring just to a boil, and pack in sterile jars. This relish may need to be drained when used or you can simmer only the raw carrots and cabbage until liquid is reduced, add the uncooked corn, and simmer 10 minutes longer before sealing. Corn will toughen if overcooked.

Yield: approximately 3 cups

GOLDEN RELISH

Ingredients:

6 LONG, SLIM RIPE CUCUMBERS

5 MEDIUM ONIONS, WHITE OR YELLOW

¼ CUP COARSE SALT

WATER

2 CUPS CIDER VINEGAR

1 CUP SUGAR

2 TEASPOONS TURMERIC

1 TEASPOON MUSTARD SEED

½ TEASPOON DRY MUSTARD

¼ TEASPOON CINNAMON

¼ TEASPOON CLOVES

¼ TEASPOON ALLSPICE

1. Peel and finely chop or grind the vegetables. Add the salt and water to cover. Let for stand 2 hours, rinse and drain well. Press out as much water as possible.
2. In a separate pan, combine the vinegar, sugar, turmeric, mustard seed, dry mustard, and spices and simmer, covered, for 10 minutes. Let stand while the vegetables are in the brine.
3. Add vegetables to the syrup and simmer until vegetables are tender and yellow in color. Seal in sterile jars.

Yield: approximately 2 to 3 pints

*Note: Collect the juices while grinding the vegetables for the relish. Freeze the juice in ice cube trays, store in plastic bags in the freezer, and use in soups and stews for added flavor.

UNCOOKED RELISH

Ingredients:

¼ HEAD OF CABBAGE

1 GREEN SWEET PEPPER

1 MEDIUM YELLOW ONION

2 SLENDER CUCUMBERS, PEELED AND DESEEDED

¼ CUP COARSE SALT

1 LARGE APPLE, SUCH AS GRANNY SMITH OR GOLDEN DELICIOUS, PEELED AND
 CORED

Syrup ingredients:

2 CUPS CIDER VINEGAR

1 CUP WHITE SUGAR

2 TEASPOONS MUSTARD SEED

¼ TEASPOON CELERY SEED

½ TEASPOON CLOVES

½ TEASPOON ALLSPICE

1. Grind together the vegetables, add the salt, and let it drain overnight in a cloth bag or strainer.
2. Combine the syrup ingredients in a pan large enough to hold the ground vegetables. Simmer together for 15 minutes, covered. This can be done the night before and left to steep overnight for more flavor.
3. Grind the apple and add to the syrup along with any juice. Rinse and drain the vegetables well and add to the syrup. Bring just to a boil and let cool in the pan. Store in the refrigerator in clean jars for at least 1 week before using.

Yield: depending on the size of your vegetables, you will have between 3 and 4 pints

*Note: To make this a cooked relish, cook as in the above recipe. For additional color, replace some of the green pepper with red sweet pepper. If heat is desired, grind some hot pepper with the other vegetables.

BROCCOLI SLAW RELISH

Ingredients:
12 OZ. BAG BROCCOLI SLAW
1 MEDIUM ONION
1 RED SWEET PEPPER, SLICED (OPTIONAL)
1 OR MORE SMALL HOT PEPPERS (OPTIONAL)
2 TABLESPOONS COARSE SALT

Syrup ingredients:
¾ CUP WATER
½ CUP VINEGAR
½ CUP SUGAR, BROWN OR WHITE
2 TEASPOONS MUSTARD SEED
¼ TEASPOON CLOVES
¼ TEASPOON ALLSPICE
½ TEASPOON TURMERIC (OPTIONAL—WILL GIVE THE RELISH A GOLDEN COLOR)
GARLIC POWDER, CAYENNE PEPPER, CELERY SEED, AND MINCED PARSLEY (OPTIONAL)

1. For easier grinding, first chop the slaw to cut up the long shreds. Grind the slaw and onion and, if you want additional color, grind several slices of red sweet pepper. For heat, grind up the hot pepper. You should have 3 to 4 cups after grinding the vegetables.
2. Mix in the salt. Let stand for 1 hour, then rinse well in batches using a fine mesh strainer. Taste for saltiness, and if too salty, soak in cold water for 30 minutes and rinse again. Press out as much water as possible.
3. Combine the syrup ingredients and simmer for 10 minutes, covered. Let stand while the vegetables are salting.

4. Add the vegetables to the syrup and cook at a simmer, uncovered, until the vegetables are tender and liquid is reduced, about 2 hours. Add water or vinegar if too dry before cooking is done.

Yield: approximately 3 to 4 cups

*Note: Other vegetables, such as cucumbers, can be added when grinding for a different taste.

WINTER RELISH

Ingredients:

3 LONG, SLENDER CUCUMBERS

3 MEDIUM TO LARGE YELLOW OR WHITE ONIONS

1 SMALL HEAD CABBAGE, OR HALF A LARGE HEAD

3 GREEN PEPPERS, OR 1 RED AND 2 GREEN

2 LARGE GARLIC CLOVES, OR TO TASTE

3 LARGE CARROTS

¼ CUP COARSE SALT

Syrup ingredients:

1 ½ CUPS CIDER VINEGAR

½ CUP BROWN SUGAR

½ CUP WHITE SUGAR

1 TABLESPOON MUSTARD SEED

½ TEASPOON CLOVES

½ TEASPOON ALLSPICE

½ TEASPOON TURMERIC (OPTIONAL—WILL GIVE RELISH A GOLDEN COLOR)

¼ TO ½ TEASPOON CAYENNE PEPPER (OPTIONAL)

1. Peel, quarter, and seed the cucumbers. Peel the onions. Trim the cabbage and wash and remove the seeds from the peppers. Peel the garlic. Scrape or peel the carrots. Cut all vegetables into small chunks and mix together. You will have about 5 ½ quarts of cut vegetables. Grind them and drain well. Collect the juice and save it to flavor soups or stews.
2. Mix the ground vegetables with the salt, add water to cover, and soak for 1 hour. Drain well by batches in a strainer, pressing water out gently. Put in a kettle.
3. Add the syrup ingredients, mix well, and cook at a simmer about 30 minutes, or until vegetables are tender and the relish is not too runny. Add water or vegetable juice if it becomes too dry.

Yield: approximately 4 pints

ANOTHER GREEN TOMATO RELISH

Ingredients:

1 ROUNDED QT. ROUGHLY CHOPPED GREEN TOMATOES

¼ CUP COARSE SALT

½ SMALL HEAD OF CABBAGE

1 GREEN PEPPER

1 SMALL RED SWEET PEPPER

3 MEDIUM ONIONS

GARLIC CLOVES (OPTIONAL)

HOT PEPPERS (OPTIONAL)

Syrup ingredients:

2 CUPS CIDER VINEGAR

½ TO 1 CUP BROWN OR WHITE SUGAR

1 TABLESPOON MUSTARD SEED

1 TEASPOON CLOVES

1 TEASPOON ALLSPICE

½ TEASPOON TURMERIC, CAYENNE PEPPER, GARLIC POWDER, AND CELERY SEED
    (OPTIONAL)

1. **Day 1**: Prepare the green tomatoes. Wash, cut up, grind, discarding the juice, and measure. There should be about 2 cups ground tomatoes. Add the salt, mix, and drain overnight in a strainer, colander lined with paper towels, or in a cloth bag.
2. **Day 2**: Grind together the cabbage, green pepper, red sweet pepper, and onion (add garlic cloves and hot pepper here, if using). Drain and set aside excess juices and measure the vegetables. There should be about 4 ½ to 5 cups.
3. In a kettle, combine all the vegetables and the reserved juice. Add the syrup ingredients and mix well. Cook, uncovered, at a simmer until the vegetables are tender and the liquid is reduced, about 1 ½ hours. If relish becomes too dry, add a little water or the vegetable juice. Seal in sterile jars.

Yield: approximately 4 pints

UNCOOKED FRESH RELISH

Ingredients:

½ SMALL HEAD OF CABBAGE

1 LARGE SWEET ONION

1 SMALL GREEN PEPPER

1 LARGE, SLIM CUCUMBER

1 LARGE COOKING APPLE

2 TO 4 TABLESPOONS COARSE SALT

Syrup ingredients:

2 CUPS CIDER VINEGAR

1 CUP BROWN SUGAR

1 TEASPOON CELERY SEED

1 TEASPOON MUSTARD SEED

¼ TEASPOON CLOVES

¼ TEASPOON ALLSPICE

1. Prepare the vegetables. Trim and cut the cabbage into pieces. Peel and coarsely chop the onion. Wash the pepper, cut in quarters, remove the seeds, and chop coarsely. Peel the cucumber, cut in quarters lengthwise, remove the seeds, and cut into small pieces. Peel, core, and cut the apple into small pieces.
2. Mix the vegetables and grind. Mix in the salt and let stand overnight in a bowl, covered.
3. In a pan large enough to hold the ground vegetables, mix the vinegar, sugar, celery and mustard seed, and spices, bring to a boil, and let stand overnight, covered.
4. The next day, drain and rinse the vegetables, squeezing out the water. If too salty, soak in freshwater for 1 hour and drain well. Combine the vegetables and syrup and let stand at room temperature overnight. Place in clean jars and store in the refrigerator.

Yield: approximately 2 pints

*Note: For more color, use half of a small green pepper and half of a red. Adding some carrot will also give additional color to the relish.

MINUTE RELISH

Ingredients:

FRESH VEGETABLES, AS MUCH AS YOU WISH

COARSE SALT, ¼ TEASPOON FOR EACH CUP OF GROUND VEGETABLES

VINEGAR, ¼ CUP PER CUP OF VEGETABLES

SUGAR, BROWN OR WHITE, 1 TABLESPOON PER CUP

SPICES OF YOUR CHOOSING, ½ TEASPOON PER CUP

GARLIC POWDER, CAYENNE PEPPER, MUSTARD SEED, OR CELERY SEED TO TASTE

1. Select crisp, fresh vegetables and grind coarsely. Drain and measure.
2. Add the other ingredients for each cup of measured ground vegetables. Mix well and store in clean jars or a bowl in the refrigerator. Your yield depends on how many cups of vegetables you grind. This relish is best made in small amounts and used in short time.

HOT PEPPER RELISH

Ingredients:

1 LONG ENGLISH CUCUMBER (APPROX. 1 ¼ LBS.)

1 MEDIUM YELLOW ONION

½ CUP CHOPPED CARROTS

⅔ CUP CHOPPED CELERY (INCLUDE A FEW LEAVES)

½ TO 1 WHOLE RED SWEET PEPPER

HOT PEPPERS TO TASTE, CHOPPED. FOR A RESPECTABLY WARM RELISH, USE THESE
　　　THREE PEPPERS COMBINED:

1 JALAPENO PEPPER (APPROX. 3 ½ INCHES LONG)
1 RED CHILI (APPROX. 3 ½ INCHES LONG)
1 SERRANO PEPPER (APPROX. 2 INCHES LONG)
4 TEASPOONS COARSE SALT

Syrup ingredients:
¾ CUP CIDER VINEGAR
1 CUP RESERVED VEGETABLE JUICE AND/OR WATER
1 TABLESPOON MUSTARD SEED
¼ TO ½ TEASPOON POWDERED GARLIC OR GRIND A LARGE CLOVE FRESH GARLIC WITH
      THE VEGETABLES
¼ TEASPOON ALLSPICE
¼ TEASPOON CLOVES
CELERY SEED AND GINGER (OPTIONAL)
½ CUP SUGAR

1. Peel the cucumber, quarter lengthwise, remove any mature seeds, and chop coarsely. Peel and coarsely chop the onion. Add the carrots and celery. Core, seed, and coarsely chop the sweet pepper. Add chopped hot peppers in whatever quantity desired to add flavor and heat to your relish.
2. Mix the chopped vegetables and grind. A blender or food processor is likely to puree the vegetables too much, so use a hand or machine grinder for best results. There will be 4 to 5 cups of ground vegetables. Place them in a nonreactive bowl. Drain off as much of the juices as possible and save. Mix in the salt and let stand for 1 hour at room temperature, stirring occasionally.
3. Drain the vegetables in a sieve in batches, rinse, and drain well again, pressing out as much water as possible. Put the vegetables in a pan.
4. Add all the syrup ingredients except the sugar, mix well, and simmer, uncovered, until vegetables are almost tender and liquid is reduced, about 30 minutes. If relish becomes too dry before it is done, add water or vegetable juices in ¼-cup amounts.

5. Add the sugar. This will give a fairly sweet relish. If you wish, use less and taste for sweetness. Continue cooking for 30 minutes more.
6. Seal in sterile jars or refrigerate.

Yield: 3 to 4 half-pint jars of relish

*Serving suggestions: Spread on sandwiches. Serve with meats and sausages. Add to soups, stews, and chili. Mix into tartar sauce and salad dressings. It is also tasty added to sour cream as a dip or on baked potatoes. Add to cream cheese or a purchased cheese spread and serve as a spread for crackers or stuffed in celery sticks.

*Note: When handling hot peppers, always protect your hands with rubber gloves. Try to avoid breathing the steam from the cooking relish and be careful not to touch your eyes in case any pepper juice has gotten on your hands. Hot pepper in your eyes is not to be desired. A good scrub with table salt will help remove vegetable odors from your hands.

SCOVILLE SCALE FOR MEASURING HOT PEPPERS

One of the ways to compare hot peppers is by the Scoville scale, which measures the amount of capsaicin each type of pepper contains. The number of Scoville Heat Units (SHUs) shows the average amount of capsaicin in each type of pepper, but there is a range due to growing conditions and brand of seeds used. This list is useful when selecting the kind and amount of pepper you want to use in a pickle or relish:

Pure capsaicin	15 to 16 million SHU
Habanera pepper	100,000 to 350,000 SHU
Pequin pepper	50,000 to 100,000 SHU
Cayenne pepper	30,000 to 50,000 SHU
Serrano pepper	10,000 to 23,000 SHU
Jalapeno pepper	2,500 to 8,000 SHU
Poblano pepper	500 to 2,500 SHU
Pimento, peperoncini	100 to 500 SHU
Bell pepper	zero SHU

MINCEMEAT

For centuries, thrifty cooks made mincemeat because it is economical, tasty, and a good way to use small amounts of meats and fruits. Scraps of meat left after eating a roast were typically ground or chopped for a "mince." Spices were added as a preservative and to disguise the results of a lack of refrigeration. There usually was an abundance of dried fruits to add to the mixture, and if you were lucky, a sweetener was also available. Baked in a pie, minced meat appeared either as the main course or as a sweet to end the banquet, depending on the amount of sweetening used.

Today's homemakers, not surprisingly, are still making mincemeat. Though the costs have risen, the taste of homemade mincemeat is unequaled, and no matter when it is served, hot mincemeat is sure to be a real treat.

Try some of these recipes and then branch out on your own. Most any meats, including wild game, may be used, though beef is the most common, and many mincemeat mixtures do not include any meat at all. Your choice of fruits and spices will result in many unique taste adventures. Some brandy, rum, or other liquor is often added for additional taste, though if you do not care for that, just leave it out.

It will take only 2 cups of mincemeat for an 8-inch pie and 3 cups for a 9-inch, so quantities need not be large. And remember that mincemeat has many uses. Try it as a tasty addition to cookies, tarts, sweet rolls, and poultry stuffing, in addition to filling for pies.

Mincemeats that contain suet or meat are safer stored in the refrigerator and used in a week. If longer storage is wanted, it is best to freeze your mincemeat. Canning is safest left to commercial canneries.

MEATLESS MINCEMEAT

Ingredients:

3 FIRM, TART COOKING APPLES
½ LB. BEEF SUET
2 CUPS RAISINS
1 CUP MIXED CANDIED FRUIT
1 LARGE NAVEL ORANGE
JUICES FROM GROUND FRUIT
JUICE, CIDER, OR APPLE BRANDY (IF NEEDED)
1 CUP BROWN SUGAR
1 CUP CURRANTS
½ TEASPOON ALLSPICE
½ TEASPOON CLOVES
½ TEASPOON CINNAMON
½ TEASPOON SALT

1. Peel the apples, core, and chop coarsely. Chop the suet. Wash and squeeze dry the raisins. Grate the orange rind and remove the fruit from the pith and membranes. Mix the ingredients and grind, collecting the juices. Place the ground mixture in a large saucepan.
2. Measure the reserved juices and use another juice or brandy to make the liquid total 1 cup. Mix into the fruit.
3. Add the sugar, currants (wash and squeeze dry), spices, and salt. Mix well and cook at a simmer for 45 minutes to 1 hour, adding juice if too dry. Using a diffuser over the burned will help avoid sticking. Store in the refrigerator.

Yield: 2 to 3 pints

GREEN TOMATO MINCEMEAT

Ingredients:

4 CUPS FINELY CHOPPED GREEN TOMATOES,

2 CUPS PEELED, CORED, AND CHOPPED TART COOKING APPLES

1 ORANGE

2 CUPS RAISINS

½ CUP GROUND OR CHOPPED FINELY CANDIED FRUIT PEELS,

2 CUPS BROWN SUGAR

½ TEASPOON CLOVES

½ TEASPOON ALLSPICE

½ TEASPOON GINGER

½ TEASPOON SALT

APPLE OR ORANGE JUICE, AS NEEDED

1. Grate the orange rind and remove the white pith. Cut the fruit from between the membranes, and chop. Squeeze the juice from the membranes. Wash, squeeze dry, and chop the raisins.
2. Combine all ingredients in a heavy-bottomed pan and simmer for about 1 hour, adding fruit juices, such as apple or orange, as needed to keep from sticking. Store as above.

Yield: 2 to 3 pints

MOM'S MINCEMEAT

Ingredients:

2 CUPS LEAN BEEF (STEW MEAT WORKS BEST)

4 CUPS PEELED, CORED, AND CHOPPED TART APPLES

2 CUPS RAISINS

2 CUPS CURRANTS

1 CUP CHOPPED CITRON

1 CUP CHOPPED BEEF SUET

2 CUPS SUGAR

1 CUP CIDER OR FRUIT JUICE

1 CUP BEEF STOCK (FROM COOKING MEAT)

2 TEASPOONS SALT

1 TEASPOON NUTMEG

1 TEASPOON CLOVES

1 TEASPOON CINNAMON

1. Remove as much fat as possible from the meat and simmer in water until well done. Drain and save the broth. Mix together with the apples, raisins and currants (washed and squeezed dry), citron, and beef suet. Grind the mixture and transfer to a heavy bottomed kettle. Add sugar, cider/fruit juice, beef stock, salt, and spices. Mix well and simmer slowly for 1 hour. When the cooking time is half over, taste the mincemeat and adjust the seasonings to your taste. If more liquid is needed, add juice, brandy, or rum a little at a time. Store as above

Yield: approximately 6 pints

FRUITED MINCEMEAT

Ingredients:
1 CUP CHOPPED BEEF SUET
1 CUP CHOPPED DRIED APRICOTS
1 CUP CHOPPED DRIED PEACHES
1 CUP CHOPPED CARROTS
1 CUP RAISINS
½ CUP DICED CITRON
4 LARGE, TART APPLES
3 NAVEL ORANGES
2 CUPS SUGAR, BROWN OR WHITE
1 CUP CIDER OR FRUIT JUICE
1 TEASPOON CINNAMON
½ TEASPOON CLOVES
½ TEASPOON ALLSPICE
½ TEASPOON MACE
½ TEASPOON GINGER

1. Grind together the suet, apricots and peaches (you may also use mixed dried fruit instead), carrots, raisins (washed and squeezed dry), citron, apples (peeled, cored, and chopped), and oranges (grate the rind, remove the fruit from the pith and membranes, squeeze the juice out, and chop the fruit). Transfer the ground mixture to a large heavy-bottomed pan and add the rest of the ingredients, including the orange juice and rind.
2. Mix well and simmer until well blended and fruits are tender, about 1 to 1 ½ hours. Add additional juice, a little at a time, if mixture becomes too dry. Store as above.

Yield: 5 to 6 pints

WILD GAME MINCEMEAT

Ingredients:

3 cups cooked and chopped lean meat (such as moose, deer, or elk)

1 cup chopped beef suet

3 tart apples

1 cup raisins

1 cup currants

½ cup diced citron

1 cup diced mixed candied fruit peel

2 cups apples juice

1 ½ cups brown sugar

1 tablespoon cinnamon

1 teaspoon ginger

½ teaspoon cloves

½ teaspoon allspice

½ teaspoon mace

½ teaspoon salt

1. Peel and core the apples. Wash and squeeze dry the raisins and currants. Mix and grind these together with the meat, suet, and candied fruit peel. Transfer to a heavy-bottomed pan.

2. Add the apple juice, sugar, cinnamon, ginger, spices, and salt. Mix well and simmer until thickened, adding juice a little at a time, if needed. At the end, you may wish to add brandy or rum for extra flavor. Store as above.

   Yield: approximately 4 cups of mincemeat depending on how long it is cooked

*Note: Candied fruit peels are most often available around Christmastime when they are marketed for making fruitcake, but larger stores may have them all year.

MEAT, FISH, AND EGGS

Pickling and brining, along with smoking and drying, were some of the earliest methods of preserving food before the days of refrigeration. Herbs and spices were added to scraps of raw meat to make sausages, which could then be smoked. Hams were salted and smoked and could be sliced all winter. If the summer had been bountiful, winter then became a time of good eating. Many of these old traditional ways of preserving can be done on a smaller scale in the modern kitchen, but for the sake of safety, do not attempt long storage of these items. Plan to use them within the time indicated with each recipe and do store in the refrigerator or freezer.

CORNED BEEF BRISKET

Ingredients:

3 cups water

¾ cup coarse salt

2 tablespoons brown sugar

3 to 4 large garlic cloves

½ teaspoon paprika

1 to 2 tablespoons mixed pickling spices

2 bay leaves

1 quart cold water

saltpeter mixture (see note at end)

5- to 6-lb. piece of beef brisket, well trimmed

1. In a large pan, boil the 3 cups of water and add the salt. Stir to dissolve and add the brown sugar, garlic cloves (peeled and crushed or minced), paprika, pickling spices, bay leaves, cold water and saltpeter mixture. Let cool to room temperature.
2. Place the meat in a refrigerator container with a tight lid. It should be large enough to allow the brining solution to get to all surfaces. Pour on the brining mixture and add water to cover completely. Weigh down with a small plate. Let marinate for at least 2 weeks or more, turning occasionally and keeping submerged.
3. Remove the meat and rinse well. Simmer gently in freshwater until done, about 3 hours depending on the size and thickness of the meat. Cool in the liquid to serve cold or serve hot with mustard, slicing across the grain of the meat. The meat should be cooked as soon as it is done brining and used within a few days. Freeze for longer storage.

*Note: Boneless pork roast or a small fresh ham can be brined instead of the beef. Adjust the brining time to the thickness of the meat. To keep the red color of the finished corned beef, dissolve $\frac{1}{4}$ teaspoon saltpeter in $\frac{1}{4}$ cup warm water and set aside. Saltpeter can be found at drugstores, but if unavailable, the taste will not suffer, just the color.

SAUERBRATEN

~◦◦◦◦~

This is a preserving as well as a tenderizing process for tougher cuts of beef. Today, we do not need this method for preserving, but it certainly adds to the taste and texture of any tougher cut of meat. Pork can also be tenderized this way as well as wild game.

Marinade Ingredients:

2 ½ CUPS DRY RED WINE

2 ½ CUPS RED WINE VINEGAR

2 ½ CUPS WATER

2 ONIONS, PEELED, SLICED, AND COARSELY CHOPPED

1 SMALL LEMON, SLICED AND SEEDS REMOVED

1 CUP CHOPPED CARROT

1 CELERY STALK, CHOPPED COARSELY

WHOLE GARLIC CLOVES PEELED AND CHOPPED, TO TASTE

10 WHOLE CLOVES, CRACKED

10 WHOLE PEPPERCORNS, CRACKED

10 JUNIPER BERRIES, CRACKED

4 BAY LEAVES, BROKEN

2 TABLESPOONS BROWN SUGAR WITHOUT IODINE

2 TEASPOONS MUSTARD SEED

1. Make a marinade from the ingredients above. Heat the marinade to a boil and simmer, covered, for 10 minutes. Let stand at room temperature overnight.

Meat Ingredients:

4 TO 4 ½ LBS. BOTTOM ROUND OF BEEF (IN 2 PIECES OR IN 1 PIECE IF YOU HAVE LARGE CONTAINERS FOR MARINATING AND ROASTING. A PIECE NO MORE THAN 2 TO 3 INCHES THICK IS BEST.)

SALT

PEPPER

ORANGE MARMALADE (OPTIONAL)

1. Immerse meat in the marinade. Refrigerate for 3 to 4 days, turning twice a day.
2. Dry the meat, salt and pepper, and brown on all sides in olive or vegetable oil. Place in a large covered roaster pan.

3. Strain the marinade and heat the liquid to a boil. Pour the solids over and around the meat and add enough boiling liquid to half cover. Roast, covered, at 325°F for about 3 hours or until tender. Add liquid if necessary to prevent drying.

4. Remove the meat and keep warm. Strain the marinade, discarding the solids. Skim off fat from the surface; add any unused marinade, and boil, uncovered, to reduce for about 15 minutes. Taste, and if too sour, add several spoonfuls of orange marmalade to sweeten and serve as a sauce with the meat. This will make a large amount of sauce. To speed up the making, use just part of the marinade. Plan on cooking your sauerbraten when it is done marinating and use leftovers in a few days or freeze.

*Note: This recipe makes a large amount of sauerbraten. The recipe can easily be cut in half or you may want to freeze the extra in a large-enough container to allow it to be covered with stained marinade.

COUNTRY STYLE SAUSAGE

Ingredients:

2 LBS. LEAN GROUND PORK

1 TO 2 TEASPOONS SALT

DRY POULTRY SEASONING MIX THAT INCLUDES SAGE

¼ TO ½ CUP WATER

1. Season the meat to taste with the salt and good-quality poultry seasoning mix.
2. Add the water and mix together lightly, making sure to distribute the seasonings.
3. Form into patties and fry until cooked through. Use within 2 days or freeze.

FRENCH SAUSAGE

Ingredients:

1 ½ LBS. LEAN GROUND PORK

2 TEASPOONS SALT

⅛ TEASPOON FRESHLY GROUND PEPPER

⅛ TEASPOON FINELY CRUMBLED BAY LEAF

ALLSPICE, TO TASTE

OREGANO, TO TASTE

SAGE, TO TASTE

1 LARGE CLOVE GARLIC, PEELED AND CRUSHED, OR ⅛ TEASPOON GARLIC POWDER

¼ CUP BRANDY, JUICE, OR OTHER LIQUID OF CHOICE

¼ CUP WATER

1. Mix all ingredients together lightly, being sure to distribute the seasonings.
2. Form the meat into patties and fry until cooked through. Use within 2 days or freeze.

PICKLED EGGS 1

Ingredients:

½ CUP WHITE VINEGAR

3 CUPS WATER

1 TEASPOON SALT

SPICE BAG WITH 1 SMALL DRY RED PEPPER AND 1 TABLESPOON MIXED PICKLING
     SPICES (P. 192)

6 SHELLED HARD-BOILED EGGS, HOT

1. Simmer together the vinegar, water, salt, and spice bag, covered, for 10 minutes.
2. If you prefer, the spices may be left loose in the brine.
3. Pack the hot eggs in a hot clean quart jar, cover with liquid, and refrigerate for 3 to 4 days before serving. Use a large-enough jar to allow room for the spice bag, if using. Carefully rotate the eggs every day to distribute the seasoning. Use the eggs within 5 or 6 days of making.

PICKLED EGGS 2

Ingredients:
HARD-BOILED EGGS (AS MANY AS YOU LIKE)
LIQUID FROM ONE OF THE PICKLED BEETS RECIPES (P. 90)

1. Hard-boil and shell as many eggs as desired. Place the hot eggs in a jar and cover with boiling beet pickle liquid. Refrigerate for several days before serving. Move the eggs around in the jar every day to avoid white spots. The eggs will add more color as long as they are stored and the white will become firmer but plan to use them within a week.

*Note: These eggs are especially colorful served as deviled eggs or sliced.

PICKLED EGGS 3

Ingredients:
1 CAN BEETS
WATER
½ CUP VINEGAR
½ CUPS SUGAR
1 CINNAMON STICK, BROKEN
½ TEASPOON WHOLE CLOVES
6 TO 8 HOT HARD-BOILED EGGS, PEELED

1. Drain off the juice from the beets and use the vegetables in some other recipe. Add enough water to the juice to make 1 cup.
   Add the vinegar, sugar, cinnamon, and whole cloves. Simmer, uncovered, for 10 minutes.
2. Pour the liquid over the hot eggs. Let marinate for several days before serving. This method will not give the depth of color obtained from using beet pickle juice but it will give the eggs a very good taste. Plan on using the eggs within a week.

DILLED SHRIMP

Ingredients:
1 lb. cooked shrimp
1 teaspoon Worcestershire sauce
juice of 1 lemon
hot sauce, to taste
1 tablespoon dill weed, finely chopped, or 1 teaspoon dried dill weed
½ teaspoon onion powder

1. Clean the cooked shrimp, gently squeeze out any liquid, and lightly toss with a sauce made from the remaining ingredients.
2. Marinate for several hours in the refrigerator, drain, and serve cold. Do not plan to store them any extra time since the lemon juice will continue to cook the shrimp and toughen them.

*Note: When fresh dill weed is in season, it can be washed, finely chopped, and frozen for later use.

PICKLED SHRIMP

Ingredients:

2 LBS. RAW SHRIMP

SEVERAL CELERY TOPS, CHOPPED

2 ROUNDED TABLESPOONS MIXED PICKLING SPICES

1 TABLESPOON COARSE SALT

1 ONION, SLICED

SEVERAL BAY LEAVES, BROKEN

1 CUP CANOLA OIL

½ CUP WHITE VINEGAR

1 TEASPOON SALT

1 TEASPOON CELERY SEED

1 TEASPOON MUSTARD SEED

HOT SAUCE, TO TASTE

GARLIC POWDER, TO TASTE

1. Wash the shrimp and put into a kettle of water to cover along with the celery tops, pickling spices, and salt.
2. Bring to a boil and cook only until the shrimp turn orange, about 3 minutes, depending on the size of the shrimp. Drain, cool, and clean the shrimp.
3. Layer the shrimp in a casserole dish with the onion and bay leaves. Mix the remaining ingredients and pour over the shrimp. Refrigerate, and let marinate for several hours, stirring several times.
4. Drain and serve cold. These shrimp will keep in the refrigerator for several days but will gain a stronger flavor over time and could get tougher due to the vinegar's acid.
5. This recipe can be made using frozen cooked shrimp, too. Thaw them in cold water and gently squeeze out any liquid before completing the recipe.

PICKLED HERRING 1

Ingredients:

4 SALT HERRINGS

2 MEDIUM ONIONS

1 ¾ CUPS CIDER VINEGAR

⅓ CUP SUGAR

2 TABLESPOONS MIXED WHOLE SPICES OF YOUR CHOICE (PEPPERCORNS, WHOLE ALL-
    SPICE, BROKEN BAY LEAVES, ETC.)

1. Remove the heads and tails of the herring, clean the insides, and remove the skin. Cut crosswise at 1-inch intervals and carefully remove the meat on each side from the bones. Soak the meat in cold water for 24 hours in the refrigerator, covered.
2. Gently squeeze any water from the meat. Layer in one bowl or several glass jars with the peeled and slice onions. In a pan, mix together the vinegar, sugar, and spices. Heat and simmer, covered, for 5 minutes. Let steep overnight for added flavor.
3. Pour the room temperature brine over the fish and onions. Steep, covered, in the refrigerator several days before serving.

Keeps up to 2 months.

PICKLED HERRING 2

Ingredients:

1 LARGE OR 2 SMALLER SALT HERRINGS

1 MEDIUM RED ONION

6 TO 8 WHOLE ALLSPICE, CRUSHED

¾ CUP WHITE VINEGAR

¼ CUP WATER

¼ CUP SUGAR

½ TEASPOON PEPPERCORNS, WHITE OR BLACK, CRACKED

2 BAY LEAVES, BROKEN

DILL WEED, FRESH OR DRIED, CHOPPED, OR TO TASTE FOR SERVING

1. Prepare and soak the herring as in the previous recipe (p. 172).
2. Squeeze the water from the herring and arrange in one layer in a flat glass dish and top with peeled and sliced onion. Combine the rest of the ingredients, except the dill weed, in a pan and simmer together, covered, for 15 minutes. Let steep at room temperature overnight.
3. Pour the cool syrup over the herring. Let marinate overnight, or longer, in the refrigerator, covered. Drain for serving and sprinkle with dill weed. The herring will keep in the marinade for several weeks but will gain a stronger taste, so experiment to determine how long you want to leave it.

*Note: The marinade may be strained before pouring over the herring, but there will be more flavor if the seasonings are left in it.

SEASONING
SAUCES

Many of the seasoning sauces found on supermarket and specialty shop shelves can be made at home, and many made at home will never be found for sale. For quick individual seasoning and for a taste that cannot be purchased anywhere, keep a selection of these sauces on hand.

Such sauces also include a great variety of the special fruit sauces, chutneys, tomato-based sauces, and others found in earlier chapters. This chapter presents a group of sauces that are usually used to directly season foods by becoming part of a recipe rather than by being served alongside other foods.

HOT RED PEPPER SAUCE

Ingredients:

AN ASSORTMENT OF HOT RED PEPPERS OF CHOICE, YIELDING ABOUT 2 CUPS CHOPPED
PEPPERS (SEE P. 157 FOR THE CHART ON THE HEAT OF PEPPERS)

1 LARGE GARLIC CLOVE, OR MORE TO TASTE

1 TEASPOON FRESH HORSERADISH, GRATED (OR PREPARED WITHOUT ADDED CREAM)

⅓ CUP VINEGAR

2 TABLESPOONS SUGAR

1 TEASPOONS COARSE SALT

1. Wash, seed, and coarsely chop enough peppers to measure about 2 rounded cups. Protect your hands with rubber gloves while doing this. Peel and slice the garlic. Simmer the garlic and peppers in water to just cover, until soft.
2. Puree these together with the remaining ingredients in a blender or food processor. Process until well blended and transfer to a saucepan. Simmer for 10 minutes, stirring often.
3. Seal in sterile jars for longer storage, store in the refrigerator, or freeze in ice cube trays, pop out, and store in plastic bags in the freezer.

Yield: you will have around 1 to 1 ½ cups of sauce depending on the size of the peppers you use and how long you cook the sauce. This sauce may also be made with hot green peppers. A mixture of pepper colors will work but the sauce will be a muddy color.

*Note: A different hot pepper sauce may be found in the chapter "Starting with Canned Goods," page 90.

MUSHROOM KETCHUP

Ingredients:

1 LB. VERY FRESH SMALL WHITE MUSHROOMS

1 SMALL ONION

½ CUP WHITE WINE VINEGAR

1 SMALL GARLIC CLOVE

2 TABLESPOONS MINCED CELERY

1 TEASPOON SALT

¼ TO ½ TEASPOON FRESH GROUND PEPPER (OR A PINCH OF CAYENNE PEPPER)

1 TABLESPOON SUGAR

2 TABLESPOONS MIXED PICKLING SPICES, TIED IN A CLOTH BAG (P. 192)

JUICE OF ½ LEMON

1. Wash, trim, and cut the mushrooms into quarters. Peel and coarsely chop the onion.
2. Peel and slice the garlic. Combine these along with the vinegar and celery in a blender or food processor and process until smooth. Transfer to a pan and add the remaining ingredients. The spices should be confined in a bag or tea caddy, as you will not want them in the finished catsup.
3. Simmer gently, stirring often, for 30 to 40 minutes. Remove and squeeze out the spice bag. Seal in sterile jars or refrigerate. Depending on how thick you want your sauce, there will be around 1 cup.

ANCHOVY SAUCE

Ingredients:

1 LB. SALTED ANCHOVIES, OR ENOUGH CANNED TO EQUAL 1 LB. (NOT PACKED IN OIL
    OR SEASONINGS, IF POSSIBLE)

½ CUP WATER

2 TABLESPOONS CIDER VINEGAR

½ TEASPOON MACE

½ TEASPOON POWDERED ONION

½ TEASPOON POWDERED GARLIC

PINCH OF CAYENNE PEPPER, OR MORE TO TASTE

1. Rinse the anchovies well, drain, and combine in a blender or food processor with the remaining ingredients. Puree until smooth, strain, and discard anything what will not strain easily.
2. Simmer for 30 minutes, stirring often, and add water as needed to avoid sticking. Cool and store in the refrigerator.

Yield: approximately 1 cup depending on thickness

*Note: Anchovy sauce is a tasty addition to deviled eggs. Or add to sour cream or cream cheese for a dip or to spread on crackers. Water-packed sardines may be processed in the same way or experiment with water-packed tuna and salmon. The recipe can easily be cut in half.

PREPARED HORSERADISH

Ingredients:

FIRM, FRESH HORSERADISH ROOT

WHITE VINEGAR

SALT

1. Buy firm, fresh horseradish roots in whatever quantity you wish. Since the sauce will freeze well, it is more efficient to process a larger amount at once if you will be using a lot in about a year.

2. First peel the root. It may then be left whole and grated by hand or chopped and ground but the best way of processing is in a blender or food processor.

3. To process, first chop the horseradish fairly finely. Then process about 1 to 2 cups of horseradish at a time using white vinegar for liquid. You want a fairly smooth sauce but not pureed horseradish. Drain vinegar from the processed root and use with the next batch. When all cubes have been processed, add enough of the used vinegar so that the sauce is moist but not soupy. Add ¼ teaspoon salt for each cup of processed horseradish.

4. Pack in sterile jars or freezer containers. Store in the refrigerator or freezer. When the sauce starts to turn dark, discard and start a new container. This sauce cannot be sealed in jars since no heat is involved in the processing.

*Note: Processing horseradish is likely to affect your sinuses, so be prepared with tissues and try to avoid breathing the fumes.

DARK SAUCE

Ingredients:

1 CUP CIDER VINEGAR

2 LARGE ONIONS

2 TABLESPOONS MUSHROOM KETCHUP (P. 176)

2 TABLESPOONS ANCHOVY SAUCE (P. 177)

1 TABLESPOON MOLASSES OR SORGHUM

1 GARLIC CLOVE

1 TEASPOON CLOVES

½ TEASPOON CRUSHED DRY CHILIES, OR TO TASTE

½ TEASPOON COARSE SALT

½ TEASPOON FRESH GROUND BLACK PEPPER

1. Combine all of the ingredients in a blender or food processor. Process until smooth and simmer, uncovered, for 10 minutes, stirring often. If the sauce is thinner than you like, continue cooking to the desired thickness.
2. Chill and store in the refrigerator for several weeks or freeze.

Yield: about ¾ cup finished sauce.

HERB ESSENCE

Ingredients:

2 CUPS BOILING WATER

6 TABLESPOONS DRIED HERBS (ONE HERB OR A MIXTURE)

1. Pour the boiling water over the dried herbs. Allow to stand, covered, overnight.
2. Bring to a boil and let stand overnight again.
3. Strain through a cloth or very fine strainer and store in the refrigerator or freezer as ice cubes.

*Note: Select often-used herbs and use to season sauces, soups, stews, or dishes where the flavor, but not appearance, of herbs is wanted. Onion, garlic, or lemon may be added during the steeping process. For even more flavor, allow to stand in a cool dark place for several days before straining. Stir each day.

MUSTARDS

These are mustards of authority. Used generously, they will none too gently lift the top right off your head, clear the sinuses, and give all the impression of a volcanic eruption. Used with discretion, they offer a marvelous change from the pale imitations to be found on grocery shelves. All will keep for several months in a tightly covered, nonreactive container in the refrigerator. Since there is no heat used in processing, they cannot be sealed in jars for storage.

BASIC MUSTARD

This is a very forceful mustard.

Ingredients:

1–3 OZ. CAN DRY MUSTARD

2 TABLESPOONS SUGAR

2 TEASPOONS SALT

5 TABLESPOONS CIDER VINEGAR

2 TEASPOONS WORCESTERSHIRE SAUCE OR DARK SAUCE (P. 179)

2 TABLESPOONS CANOLA OIL, OR OTHER VEGETABLE OIL

FEW DROPS HOT PEPPER SAUCE

1. Blend together the dry mustard, sugar, and salt.
2. Slowly add the vinegar, Worcestershire sauce, canola oil, and hot sauce. Mix well to a smooth paste, adding enough water, ¼ to ⅓ cup, to make a mixture of the desired consistency. The mixture will thicken a bit as it chills so make it a little runny to start out.

3. Store in the refrigerator in a nonmetal container. It keeps well for a considerable time, at least several months.

   Yield: approximately 1 cup

   *Note: Onion or garlic powder may be added as well as rubbed dried herbs for a different taste. For long refrigerator storage, the powders are safest.

QUICK HOT MUSTARD

Ingredients:
¼ CUP DRY MUSTARD POWDER
¼ CUP WATER
1 TEASPOON SUGAR
¼ TEASPOON CLOVES
¼ TEASPOON SALT

1. Mix all the dry ingredients and add vinegar, a little at a time, until the desired thickness.
2. Store tightly covered in the refrigerator.
3. This is a very small batch of mustard and might be a good way to start your mustard-making experience.

ITALIAN MUSTARD

Ingredients:
¾ CUP DRY WHITE WINE, SUCH AS PINOT GRIGIO
2 TEASPOONS DRIED CHOPPED ONIONS
2 CLOVES GARLIC
1 TABLESPOON MIXED ITALIAN HERBS
3 OZ. BOX DRY MUSTARD
¼ TEASPOON SALT

1. Peel and chop the garlic cloves. In a small pan, combine the garlic with the white wine, chopped onion, and Italian herbs, which have been rubbed in your hand to release their flavor. Simmer, covered, for 15 minutes. Do not boil. Remove from the heat and let cool to room temperature. Let stand overnight to steep, if possible. Strain through a fine sieve into a spouted measuring cup.
2. In a bowl, combine the mustard and salt. Slowly add the strained wine and beat until smooth. If too thick, add a little water. Store in a nonmetal container in the refrigerator. It will keep for several months.

   Yield: approximately 1 cup

DIJON-STYLE MUSTARD

Ingredients:

1 CUP DRY WHITE WINE

1 MEDIUM YELLOW ONION

2 GARLIC CLOVES

3 TO 4 OZ. CAN DRY MUSTARD

2 TABLESPOONS SUGAR

2 TABLESPOONS CANOLA OR OTHER VEGETABLE OIL

1 TEASPOON COARSE SALT

A FEW DROPS HOT PEPPER SAUCE (OPTIONAL)

1. Combine the white wine, onion (peeled and finely chopped), and garlic (peeled and minced or crushed) in a small pan. Simmer, covered, for 10 minutes and let cool to room temperature. Letting steep overnight will add flavor. Strain into a spouted measuring cup.
2. In a bowl, combine the dry mustard and strained wine. Beat to mix well and add the sugar, oil, and salt (and hot sauce, if using).
3. Refrigerate in a nonmetal container. It will keep for several months.

Yield: approximately 1 cup

HORSERADISH MUSTARD

Add 2 to 3 tablespoons of Prepared Horseradish (p. 178) to any of the above mustards and mix well. Start with less and taste before adding all the horseradish.

HOT SWEET AND SPICY MUSTARD

Ingredients:

4 OZ. DRY MUSTARD

½ CUP BROWN SUGAR

½ TEASPOON CLOVES

½ TEASPOON GINGER

½ TEASPOON CINNAMON

½ TEASPOON SALT

CIDER VINEGAR

2 TABLESPOONS HONEY

1 TABLESPOON VEGETABLE OIL

1. Mix together the dry mustard, brown sugar, and spices in a bowl. Add cider vinegar, 1 tablespoon at a time, until mustard is almost the desired consistency. Blend in the remaining ingredients and adjust the thickness.
2. Store in a nonmetal container in the refrigerator. Chill before serving.

Yield: 1 generous cup

*Note: Molasses may be used instead of honey. Orange juice may be used instead of, or in addition to, the vinegar. The finely grated rind of one orange can also be added. If you prefer a less sweet mixture, add less of the sugar, taste, and adjust.

COOKED MUSTARD

This is a very mild mustard and a good place for experimentation.

Ingredients:

4 TABLESPOONS DRY MUSTARD

¼ CUP CIDER VINEGAR

1 TEASPOON SUGAR, BROWN OR WHITE

⅛ TEASPOON SALT

1 EGG YOLK, BEATEN

2 TABLESPOONS WATER OR ORANGE JUICE

⅛ TEASPOON TURMERIC

⅛ TEASPOON CLOVES

CAYENNE PEPPER (OPTIONAL—TO ADD MORE HEAT)

1. Mix the dry mustard, vinegar, sugar, and salt, and let stand for 2 hours.
2. Beat the egg yolk with the water or orange juice, turmeric, and cloves. Combine with the first mixture.
3. In the top of a double boiler, cook over hot water, stirring constantly, until thick. Store in the refrigerator and use within 2 or 3 weeks.

Yield: approximately ½ cup

*Optional additions: onion or garlic powder, herbs of choice, grated citrus rind, Worcestershire sauce

SEASONED
VINEGARS

These vinegars are a great convenience. They keep a long time and will give instant flavoring to sauces and salad dressings. Most call for white or distilled vinegar, but white wine and cider vinegars can also be used for variety. Be sure to store them tightly covered in non-metal containers and in a cool dark place. There will be more flavor in your vinegars if they are allowed to stand in a cool dark place for a week before straining. When simmered in a tightly covered pan, you should have almost the same amount of seasoned vinegar as the plain vinegar you started with, but some seasonings will absorb more vinegar than others. Small decorative bottles would make for a nice gift presentation.

SPICED VINEGAR 1

Ingredients:

2 CUPS WHITE VINEGAR

2 TABLESPOONS MIXED SPICES OF CHOICE

1 TEASPOON SALT

1. In a saucepan, mix all ingredients and bring to a boil. Immediately lower the heat and simmer, tightly covered, for 10 minutes.
2. Allow to cool in the pan overnight. Strain and bottle for storage.

SPICED VINEGAR 2

Ingredients:

2 CUPS WHITE VINEGAR

¼ CUP WHITE SUGAR

1 TABLESPOON BLACK PEPPERCORNS

1 SMALL CINNAMON STICK, BROKEN

1 CLOVE GARLIC, PEELED AND CRUSHED

1 TEASPOON CRUSHED DRIED GINGER

1 TEASPOON MUSTARD SEED

1 TEASPOON PREPARED HORSERADISH

1 TEASPOON SALT

1 TEASPOON WHOLE CLOVE

1. In a saucepan, combine all ingredients and simmer, covered, for 20 minutes.
2. Let cool overnight, covered, and strain through a cloth or very fine sieve. Bottle for storage.

SPICED VINEGAR 3

Ingredients:

2 CUPS WHITE VINEGAR

1 TEASPOON WHOLE CLOVES

1 CINNAMON STICK, BROKEN

4 WHOLE ALLSPICE

4 CARDAMOM PODS

1 TEASPOON DRY CRACKED GINGER

1. Simmer all ingredients together in a covered pan for 20 minutes.
2. Let cool overnight, covered, and strain. Bottle for storage.

SEEDED VINEGAR

Ingredients:

2 CUPS WHITE VINEGAR OR WHITE WINE VINEGAR

3 TABLESPOONS SEEDS, SUCH AS MUSTARD, CARDAMOM, CARAWAY, CELERY, OR OTHER
SEASONING SEEDS OF CHOICE (USE ALL ONE OR A MIXTURE)

1. Whirl the seeds and part of the vinegar in a blender or food processor just long enough to break up the seeds. Pour into a saucepan and add the rest of the vinegar.
2. Bring to a simmer and cook, slowly, for 10 minutes, tightly covered. Let stand overnight and pour into a jar. Cover tightly and store in a dark place for 1 week and then strain through a cloth. Bottle for storage.

ONION VINEGAR

Ingredients:

2 CUPS WHITE VINEGAR

1 LARGE ONION, PEELED AND CHOPPED INTO SMALL PIECES

½ TEASPOON SALT

1. Heat the vinegar to a boil and add the onions and salt. Let stand for several hours to cool and then store in a covered jar for 1 week. Strain and bottle for storage. You will have about 1 ¾ cups of finished vinegar since the onions will absorb quite a bit. The strained onions could be a nice addition to many dishes.

GARLIC VINEGAR

Ingredients:

2 CUPS WHITE VINEGAR OR WHITE
WINE VINEGAR

4 TO 6 LARGE FRESH GARLIC CLOVES,
PEELED AND MINCED

¼ TEASPOON SALT

1. Heat the vinegar just to a boil and add the garlic and salt. Let stand for several hours to cool and then store in a covered jar for one week. Strain and bottle for storage.

   *Note: A mixed onion and garlic vinegar can be made with ½ of an onion and 3 cloves garlic. Herbs could be added for a different flavor.

FIRE VINEGAR

Ingredients:

2 CUPS WHITE VINEGAR

2 TABLESPOONS CRUSHED DRY CHILI PEPPERS OR MORE TO TASTE

1. Combine and bring to a boil in a tightly covered pan. Simmer for 15 minutes. Let stand for several hours to cool and store in a covered jar for 1 week, shaking every day. Strain through a cloth and bottle for storage.
2. Increase the amount of chilies for even more heat. Reheating the vinegar before straining will also strengthen the heat.

HERBED VINEGAR

Ingredients:

2 CUPS WHITE VINEGAR OR WHITE WINE VINEGAR

4 TABLESPOONS DRY HERBS, SUCH AS BASIL, OREGANO, THYME, OR YOUR FAVORITES (USED SINGLY OR IN A MIXTURE). FOR A STRONGER FLAVOR, USE ADDITIONAL HERBS. RUBBING THE HERBS IN YOUR HAND OR BRUISING THEM WITH A MORTAR AND PESTLE ALSO WILL HELP RELEASE THEIR FLAVOR BUT DO NOT GRIND THEM INTO A POWDER.

1. Combine and simmer, tightly covered, for 15 minutes. Let cool, pour into a covered jar, and let stand in a dark place for 1 week. Strain through a cloth or fine sieve and bottle for storage.

   *Note: Additions might be thin lemon rind removed with a vegetable peeler and/or a little minced onion or garlic.

ORANGE SPICED VINEGAR

Ingredients:

2 CUPS WHITE OR CIDER VINEGAR

1 TEASPOON WHOLE COVES

1 STICK CINNAMON, BROKEN

1 TEASPOON WHOLE ALLSPICE

1 TEASPOON CRUSHED DRIED GINGER

COARSELY GRATE THE RIND OF ONE LARGE ORANGE

1. Combine all ingredients and simmer, covered, for 20 minutes. Let cool and pour into a jar. Store in a cool dark place for 1 week and strain. Bottle for storage.

ORANGE SPICED DRESSING

Ingredients:

½ CUP SALAD OIL OR CHOICE

¼ TO ½ CUP ORANGE SPICED VINEGAR (ABOVE)

½ TEASPOON DRY MUSTARD

¼ CUP HONEY, OR TO TASTE

1. Combine in a jar and shake well. Serve chilled on a fruit or vegetable salad.

Yield: ¾ to 1 cup

HONEYS, TEAS, SPICES, AND POWDERS

A few extra recipes to add spice to your cooking and life.

ORANGE SPICED HONEY

Ingredients:

1 CUP CLOVER HONEY, OR OTHER MILD HONEY
ORANGE PEEL STRIPS REMOVED FROM 1 ORANGE
    WITH A VEGETABLE PEELER AND CUT INTO
    SHREDS WITH A KNIFE
1 SMALL CINNAMON STICK, BROKEN
½ TEASPOON WHOLE ALLSPICE
½ TEASPOON WHOLE CLOVES
4 CARDAMOM PODS

1. Warm the honey in a glass container in the microwave or in a small pan over low heat.
2. Pour it over the seasonings in a glass jar and leave at room temperature for 1 to 2 weeks before using.

*Note: The orange rind may be very coarsely grated instead of shredded by hand. This honey is a great addition to a fruit bowl or hot tea. Many other seasoned honeys can easily be made in the same way.

SPICED SUGAR

Ingredients:

½ TEASPOON CINNAMON

¼ TEASPOON CLOVES

⅛ TEASPOON GROUND CARDAMOM

½ CUP WHITE SUGAR

1. Mix well and store in a glass jar, covered.

*Note: Sprinkle on toast, on top of sweet breads before baking, on hot cereal, use in spice buns, or wherever a little sweetness and spice is wanted. Alter the spices to your own taste.

GINGER TEA

Ingredients:

1 CUP WATER

1 TEASPOON LEMON JUICE, OR TO TASTE

½ TO 1 TEASPOON MINCED FRESH GINGER

SUGAR OR HONEY TO TASTE

1. Boil the water and pour into a mug or cup. Add the lemon juice. Place a small strainer on the cup so that its bottom is submerged. Add the minced fresh ginger to the strainer and let steep for several minutes.
2. Remove the strainer, add sugar or honey to taste, and enjoy.

*Note: A tasty help for a mild tummy upset. Add honey for a sore throat or enjoy any time. Minced fresh ginger will keep a long time in the freezer, so it is always handy to have on hand.

A Note on Seasonings: Many of the plant seasonings you use often can be frozen for quick convenient use at any time. Just finely chop them and freeze in tightly covered containers. Some to start with are onion, garlic, fresh ginger, fresh dill weed, and parsley. Shave or break off the amount you need for any use. They will keep a long time but a year is a safe length of time.

ITALIAN MIXED HERBS

Ingredients:
½ CUP DRIED BASIL LEAVES
3 TABLESPOONS DRIED LEAF OREGANO
2 TABLESPOONS DRIED THYME LEAVES
2 TABLESPOONS DRIED LEAF ROSEMARY
2 TABLESPOONS DRIED MARJORAM LEAVES

1. Gently mix the ingredients and store tightly covered in a dark place. Use wherever mixed herbs are needed or to give an Italian flavor to meats, sausages, and sauces.

Yield: approximately ⅔ cup

MIXED PICKLING SPICES

Ingredients:

¾ CUP WHOLE ALLSPICE

½ CUP MUSTARD SEED

¼ CUP BROKEN BAY LEAF

3 TABLESPOONS CRUSHED DRIED GINGER

3 TABLESPOONS CORIANDER SEED

3 TABLESPOONS WHOLE BLACK PEPPERCORNS

3 TABLESPOONS WHOLE CLOVES

12 CINNAMON STICKS, BROKEN INTO SMALL PIECES

2 TABLESPOONS DRY CHILIES, BROKEN

⅓ TO ½ CUP WHOLE CARDAMOM PODS

2 TABLESPOONS CASSIA BUDS

1. Mix gently and store in a dark place tightly covered or in an opaque container. This makes a large amount of mixed spices, 3 to 4 cups. If you do a lot of pickling, mix it at the beginning of the season and hope to use it up. Spices do not go bad but they do loose flavor over time, so a year is about long enough to keep this mixture. The recipe can easily be cut in half and quantities of any spice can be altered to your taste.

TRADITIONAL CURRY POWDER

In the parts of the world where curry is a staple of the diet, all cooks make their own private blend of spices. Use this blend as a starting point to create your own special curry powder. Use it wherever a unique taste is wanted, such as in stews, deviled eggs, salad dressing, and even in baking.

Ingredients:

¼ CUP CORIANDER SEED

¼ CUP GROUND TURMERIC

1 LARGE CINNAMON STICK, BROKEN FINELY

1 TABLESPOON CUMIN SEEDS

1 TEASPOON CARDAMOM SEEDS, OR ½ TEASPOON GROUND CARDAMOM

1 TEASPOON WHOLE BLACK PEPPERCORNS

1 TEASPOON GROUND GINGER

½ TEASPOON WHOLE CLOVES

2 BAY LEAVES BROKEN INTO SMALL BITS

1. Place all ingredients in a flat pan and bake at 200°F for 30 minutes, stir occasionally, and watch to avoid browning.
2. Grind in a blender, food processor, or spice grinder until evenly ground. Store tightly covered.

Yield: approximately ¾ cup

QUICK CURRY POWDER

Ingredients:

1 TABLESPOON GROUND CORIANDER

2 TABLESPOONS GROUND TURMERIC

1 TEASPOON GROUND CINNAMON

1 TEASPOON GROUND CUMIN

½ TEASPOON GROUND CARDAMOM

½ TEASPOON GROUND GINGER

¼ TEASPOON GROUND CLOVES

¼ TEASPOON FRESH GROUND BLACK PEPPER

CAYENNE PEPPER (OPTIONAL—WILL MAKE A HOTTER BLEND)

1. Mix together and store tightly covered.

Yield: approximately ⅓ cup

HERB BLEND

Ingredients:

2 TEASPOONS DRIED LEAF BASIL

1 TEASPOON DRIED LEAF THYME

1 TEASPOON DRIED PARSLEY

1 TEASPOON DRIED GROUND MACE

1 TEASPOON DRIED LEAF MARJORAM

1 TEASPOON DRIED LEAF OREGANO

1 TEASPOON GROUND CLOVES

1 TEASPOON GROUND BLACK PEPPER

1 TEASPOON SALT (OPTIONAL)

½ TEASPOON DRIED LEAF SAVORY

1. Gently mix everything together and store, tightly covered, in a dark place.

Yield: ¼ to ⅓ cup

Seasoning mixes with and without salt are handy to have on hand. Following are some ideas for mixes to try. After experimenting, you can easily develop your own special blends. Always store these mixtures tightly covered in a cool dark place and use within a few months. In all mixtures, the salt is optional as is the amount of any ingredient.

Number One

Mix together:

¼ CUP SALT

½ TEASPOON DRIED LEAF OREGANO

½ TEASPOON DRIED LEAF BASIL

½ TEASPOON DRIED LEAF THYME

Number Two

Mix together:

¼ CUP SALT

2 TEASPOONS SESAME SEEDS, TOASTED

1 TEASPOON DRIED, GRATED LEMON RIND

It is easy to dry your own lemon rind. Just grate the rind from as many lemons as you wish. Spread it on a flat pan and put in a very low oven, about 220⁰F until it dries. Stir occasionally and make sure to avoid browning.

Number Three

Mix together and whir in a blender:

¼ CUP SALT

1 TEASPOON ANISE SEED

½ TEASPOON DRIED, GRATED LEMON RIND

Number Four

Mix together:

¼ CUP SALT

1 TEASPOON GARLIC POWDER

¼ TEASPOON FRESH GROUND BLACK PEPPER

¼ TEASPOON EACH DRIED LEAF BASIL, OREGANO, THYME, AND MARJORAM

Number Five

Mix together:

2 TABLESPOONS SALT

1 TEASPOON MUSTARD POWDER

¼ TEASPOON EACH DRIED LEAF THYME, SAGE, AND ROSEMARY

¼ TEASPOON GARLIC POWDER

Number Six

Mix together:

1 TABLESPOON RUBBED, DRY SAGE

¼ TEASPOON DRIED LEAF SAVORY

¼ TEASPOON DRIED DILL WEED

¼ TEASPOON DRIED LEAF THYME

¼ TEASPOON LEAF MARJORAM

¼ TEASPOON DRIED, GRATED LEMON RIND

¼ TEASPOON GROUND ALLSPICE

⅛ TEASPOON FRESH GROUND BLACK PEPPERCORNS

Number Seven

Mix together and whir in a blender:

2 TABLESPOONS SALT

¼ TEASPOON FENNEL SEED

½ TEASPOON CRUSHED DRIED CHILIES, OR ¼ TEASPOON CAYENNE

½ TEASPOON DRY LEAF OREGANO

½ TEASPOON DRY LEAF BASIL

¼ TEASPOON GARLIC POWDER

¼ TEASPOON ONION POWDER

Number Eight

Mix together and whir in a blender:

2 TABLESPOONS DRY LEAF BASIL

2 TABLESPOONS DRY LEAF OREGANO

1 TABLESPOON ANISE OR FENNEL SEED

½ TEASPOON GARLIC POWDER

½ TEASPOON DRY LEAF THYME

¼ TEASPOON FRESH GROUND BLACK PEPPER

Number Nine

Mix together and whir in a blender:

1 TABLESPOON CINNAMON

1 TEASPOON CASSIA BUDS

½ TEASPOON CLOVES

¼ TEASPOON MACE

¼ TEASPOON CARDAMOM

¼ TEASPOON ANISE SEED

A tasty addition to many baked goods.

Number Ten

Mix together:

1 TABLESPOON CINNAMON

2 TEASPOONS GINGER

2 TEASPOONS CLOVES

*Note: This seasoning is especially good on toast with sugar, with apples, and in molasses cookies.

FRENCH SPICE MIX

Ingredients:

2 TEASPOONS GROUND CORIANDER

2 TEASPOONS DRIED TARRAGON LEAVES, CRUSHED

2 TEASPOONS GROUND ALLSPICE

1 TEASPOON NUTMEG, FRESHLY GROUND IF POSSIBLE

1 TEASPOON CINNAMON

½ TEASPOON GROUND CARDAMOM

½ TEASPOON DRIED MARJORAM LEAVES, CRUSHED

½ TEASPOON CLOVES

1. Combine all ingredients and mix carefully.

    *Note: Use in marinades, stuffing, sausage, stews, and on poultry and roasts.

BASIC SPICE MIX

Mix together:

⅜ CUP GROUND WHITE PEPPER

4 TEASPOONS GRATED NUTMEG, FRESHLY GROUND IF POSSIBLE

3 TEASPOONS GROUND GINGER

½ TEASPOON GROUND CLOVES

PUMPKIN SPICE BLEND

Mix together:

½ cup ground cinnamon

2 tablespoons ground cloves

1 tablespoon ground ginger

Good in any recipe that includes pumpkin.

FIRE SPICE MIX

Mix together:

¼ cup cayenne pepper

2 tablespoons ground coriander

1 teaspoon ground cumin

1 teaspoon chili powder

1 teaspoon garlic powder

1 teaspoon onion powder

½ teaspoon paprika

1 teaspoon salt

1 teaspoon sugar

ABOUT THE AUTHOR

J anet Cooper is seventy-five years old and grew up in Madison, Wisconsin. For almost as long as she can remember, she has been involved, off and on, in some way with preserving something at some time of the year. A great deal of what she knows about preserving and canning she learned from her mother, who grew up in several small towns in Iowa and came from a Pennsylvania Dutch background. As a young girl, Janet realized that summer canning was a natural way to spend her summer vacations, and by fall, the family basement canning cupboard was full of an assortment of jams, jellies, fruits, and pickles.

After graduating from the University of Wisconsin with a degree in fine arts, Janet took to wandering the United States and other countries worldwide. She's lived from coast to coast and spent three years in Ottawa, Canada, where she taught home canning for two summers. The material she collected for that course helped her develop ideas for small-batch canning and preserving throughout all the seasons. She has touched every continent and currently resides in Fitchburg, Wisconsin.

RECIPE DIRECTORY

- Chopping board—choose one that is easy to keep clean.
- Timer
- Thermometer—a candy thermometer that clips to the side of the pan is best.
- An assortment of crocks, plastic tubs, small plastic buckets, and stone jars as needed.
- Kettles—heavy-bottomed stainless steel is best; aluminum will work but acid mixtures will pit it. Never use cast iron or chipped enamel. A 4- to 6-quart kettle will handle most of these recipes.
- Conventional strainers in various sizes with a fine mesh.
- Large strainer on a stand with a pestle to force food through or a food mill.
- Food grinder—a metal grinder with a variety of blades works well. A food processor will work but it is hard to control and get evenly ground food. Many stand mixers have a grinder attachment that will work well too.
- Blender or food processor—for pureeing mixtures. For a smooth puree, a blender or food processor will work best. If you want more texture, a handheld immersion blender works very well, and for even more texture, a potato masher will often be sufficient.
- Canning jars in a variety of sizes—standard canning jars, also known as Mason jars, come in 8 oz. half pints, 16 oz. pints, and 32 oz. quarts. A few other sizes are occasionally available but these are the most commonly used sizes. You will need these for long-term sealed storage, so buy whatever size you think suits your uses. Pints and quarts also come with standard-size tops and wide-mouth tops. Choose whichever you like. When you purchase your jars, they will come with a removable rim and an inner sealer or lid, which will stay attached to the jar until it is opened for use. The lids should not be reused but the rims can be used many times before being replaced. Replacement lids and rims are readily available at stores selling canning supplies. You may reuse jars and their lids from commercially canned foods that are not standard sizes if they are to be kept in the refrigerator. Kitchen supply stores often sell attractive containers in a variety of size and shapes. They cannot be sealed but will be nice for gifts.

INGREDIENTS

◦°◦◦◦◦◦◦◦

Ingredients are listed at the beginning of each recipe. Be sure to read completely through a recipe to make sure you have everything needed. Remember: your results can be no better than your ingredients, so a few important things to remember are included here.

Produce: Use only the freshest available, store it carefully, and use as soon as possible. Fruits should be just ripe, not soft, and vegetables crisp and firm.

Vinegar: Do not try to make your own for canning. Vinegar is a preservative and must be 4 to 5 percent acid to be effective. Some of these recipes call for white vinegar and some for cider vinegar. Each will give a distinctive color and taste but usually can be used interchangeably as personal taste dictates.

Salt: This is also a preservative, so use pure non-iodized canning or kosher salt. Table salts have iodine and additives to prevent lumping that will result in cloudy syrups. Wherever salt is used in this book, it is understood to be coarse canning or kosher salt.

Spices: Spices will not go bad over time; they will just lose some flavor when kept too long. Whole spices have a longer shelf life than ground. Therefore, buy the size container that you will use up in about a year and store each spice in a cool dark place since sunlight and heat will cause deterioration. Whole and ground spices are treated differently when used. Ground spices are added directly to a mixture and will alter the color of the finished product. Whole spices may be added directly or tied in a small fabric or cheesecloth bag and removed just before